Longman Handbooks for Language Teachers

Teaching English Pronunciation

Joanne Kenworthy

London and New York

Longman Group UK Limited
Longman House, Burnt Mill, Harlow,
Essex CM20 2JE, England
and Associated Companies throughout the world.

Published in the United States of America by
Longman Inc., New York

First published 1987
Fourth impression 1990

BRITISH LIBRARY CATALOGUING IN PUBLICATION DATA
Kenworthy, Joanne
    Teaching English pronunciation. – (Longman
    handbooks for language teachers)
    1. English language – Pronunciation –
    Study and teaching
    I. Title
    428.1   PE1137

ISBN 0-582-74621-3

LIBRARY OF CONGRESS CATALOGING IN PUBLICATION DATA
Kenworthy, Joanne.
    Teaching English pronunciation.
    (Longman handbooks for language teachers)
    Bibliography: p.
    Includes index.
    1. English language – Pronunciation – Study and
teaching.   2. English language – Study and teaching
– Foreign speakers.   3. English language –
Pronunciation by foreign speakers.   I. Title.
II. Series. PE1137.K36   1987   428.3′4′07
86-10496

ISBN 0-582-74631-3

Set in 10/12 pt Linotron Times
Produced by Longman Group (Far East) Ltd.
Printed in Hong Kong

Contents

v

Introduction

This book is intended to help teachers with an aspect of English which many view as full of perplexities – pronunciation. Teachers observe their learners trying to pronounce English and realize that something is wrong. But exactly what is wrong and why? How does one account for the fact that learners seem to vary so much? Some learners seem to have few pronunciation problems, others have a great many; some individuals progress well, others seem stranded on the proverbial plateau. And why is an individual's performance so variable? Sometimes a learner can make a sound perfectly and then, in the next instant, their performance seems to deteriorate. Why all this instability? Sometimes it seems that it is not making a sound which is difficult, but knowing when and where to use it. There are some aspects of pronunciation that seem especially elusive, such as intonation. And lastly, the question that is most important for teachers – how can the teacher help? What should be taught and how?

We will explore the answers to these questions in the two parts of this book. In Part One we will examine the basic problems and principles of teaching pronunciation. In the design of any teaching programme it is essential that the process of learning is taken into account, so we begin in Chapter 1 by looking at some basic assumptions about pronunciation learning. We also consider the goals of pronunciation teaching and the roles of teacher and learner. The notion of intelligibility is crucial to pronunciation teaching. This notion and its relevance to establishing priorities in teaching pronunciation will be explored in Chapter 2. In Chapters 3 and 4 we address the question of *how*. The suggestions given for classroom activities will be presented under two headings: first, activities for building awareness and concern for pronunciation in learners; second, ways to extend and consolidate their developing skills. In teaching pronunciation we must take account of the written form of English. There is a complex relationship between sounds and spellings and many aspects of pronunciation are not represented in the writing system, or only minimally. Chapter 5 is concerned with this facet of the learning and teaching tasks. Finally, in Chapter 6, we examine the issue of integration and how teachers can achieve 'integrated pronunciation teaching'.

Part Two focuses on the specific problems encountered by speakers of particular languages. We examine these areas of difficulty in terms of learning strategies and teaching strategies. A set of priorities will be indicated for each native language group.

Acknowledgements

I owe a great debt of gratitude to all my fellow-teachers and colleagues with whom I have had the opportunity to discuss pronunciation. I would particularly like to mention Helen Oatey, and, especially in the area of intonation, Gillian Brown, Karen Currie de Carvalho, and Vivian Cook. My sincerest thanks are due to those who read the manuscript for their extremely helpful and insightful comments on versions of the book. Finally, I wish to thank my husband, David, for all his help and encouragement.

Joanne Kenworthy

Sounds and symbols

When a symbol appears between oblique lines / /, this shows that it is a *significant sound* in English. If one of the significant sounds of English is substituted for another, we get a completely different word: For example, two of the significant sounds in English are /n/ as in 'no' and /m/ as in 'me': if we take the word 'met' and substitute /n/ for /m/ we get a completely different word – 'net'. The technical term for a significant sound is a 'phoneme'. Most of the symbols that appear between oblique lines are similar to English letter symbols (as in the two examples above), but some are specially devised symbols, such as /ŋ/ which represents the sound at the end of the words, 'si*ng*', 'ri*ng*', etc. Whenever symbols are used in the text, they will *always* be accompanied by a 'key word' with the relevant letter(s) italicized, for example /m/ as in '*m*ean'. Below is a list of the phonemes of English. (The symbols are those used by the International Phonetic Alphabet, but see the note on equivalent symbols on page xii.)

Consonants

/p/ *p*eo*p*le to*p*
/b/ a*b*out *b*ig kno*b*
/t/ *t*elevision fas*t*
/d/ an*d* rea*d* *d*o
/k/ *c*ar a*c*tion
/g/ *g*o do*g*
/tʃ/ wa*tch* *ch*ur*ch*
/dʒ/ en*j*oy *j*oke fu*dge*
/f/ *f*ast rou*gh* *f*un
/v/ tele*v*ision ha*v*e li*v*e
/θ/ *th*eatre
/ð/ *th*e *th*at *th*ese

/s/ fa*s*t *s*tory me*ss*
/z/ *z*oo storie*s* live*s*
/ʃ/ a*c*tion *sh*oe
/ʒ/ televi*s*ion
/h/ *wh*o *h*ave *h*at
/l/ *l*ive *l*unch
/r/ d*r*ive *r*ead
/m/ *m*e ca*m*e
/n/ e*n*joy a*n*d ra*n*
/ŋ/ watchi*ng* doi*ng*
/j/ *y*oga *y*es
/w/ *w*atch

Vowels

/i/ r*ea*d m*ee*t
/ɪ/ watch*i*ng b*i*t wr*i*tten
/ɛ/ television b*e*t
/a/ *a*ct
/ʌ/ f*u*n
/ɒ/ w*a*tching
/ʊ/ b*oo*k p*u*t
/ə/ television *a*bout

/ɑ/ f*a*ther h*a*rd
/ɔ/ st*o*ry c*au*ght
/u/ wh*o* d*o*ing
/ei/ pl*ay*
/ai/ *I* exc*i*te
/ɔi/ enj*oy*
/ou/ g*o*ing y*o*ga
/au/ ab*ou*t n*ow*

Note on the /r/ sound

English speakers use many different kinds of /r/. Scottish speakers use an /r/ made by striking the tongue against the roof of the mouth several times very quickly; this is like the /r/ in Italian or Spanish. Some speakers in the north of England use an /r/ produced with the back of the tongue, very like the French or German type of /r/. Many speakers use a gliding, quite vowel-like /r/, which is produced with the tongue in the middle of the mouth. This is the /r/ used in British RP. (RP stands for Received Pronunciation and is the accent of Standard British English. It shows no regional variation.)

In some accents of English (notably RP and some American accents) /r/ is not pronounced after a vowel. So words like 'car', 'far', or 'beer' have a vowel sound at the end, and a word like 'hurt' has three sounds, not four. This is known as 'r-less' pronunciation.

Note on equivalent symbols

The symbols used throughout the book are those of the International Phonetic Alphabet (IPA). For the consonants, these are the same as those used in the *Longman Dictionary of Contemporary English* (1978). For the vowels (where there are some differences) the equivalent symbols are as follows:

This book		*Longman Dictionary*
/i/	read meet	/iː/
/ɪ/	watching bit written	/ɪ/
/ɛ/	television bet	/e/
/a/	act	/æ/
/ʌ/	fun	/ʌ/
/ɒ/	watching	/ɒ/
/ʊ/	book put	/ʊ/
/ə/	television about	/ə/
/ɑ/	father hard	/ɑː/
/ɔ/	story caught	/ɔː/
/u/	who doing	/uː/
/ei/	play	/eɪ/
/ai/	I excite	/aɪ/
/ɔi/	enjoy	/ɔɪ/
/ou/	going yoga	/əʊ/
/au/	about now	/au/

Using the cassette

The cassette available with this book is for 'demonstration' – the examples of pronunciation discussed in the text are recorded on the tape. When appropriate one or two additional examples have been included. (The narrator will point this out.)

    Recorded examples are marked in the text with a cassette symbol, as shown in the margin. A reference number is also given, which is spoken on the tape before each sequence.

    Some of the sequences will be suitable for classroom use, and can serve as a model for teachers in preparing their own recorded material. The tape features both British RP and North American voices.

1

Teaching and learning pronunciation

In this chapter we will examine the role of the teacher and the role of learners. What is the nature of the task before each member of the learning-teaching partnership? A large part of this chapter will be concerned with the factors which affect pronunciation learning. It is important to examine these closely because the views teachers hold about the abilities and limitations of learners are bound to influence the priorities and schedule of events in any teaching programme they devise for them. Our other major concerns will be the goals of pronunciation teaching and the implications of 'speaking with a foreign accent'. The chapter includes a brief overview of the various aspects of English pronunciation: sounds, stress, rhythm, and intonation.

1.1 The teacher's role

Helping learners hear

Part of the role of the teacher is to help learners perceive sounds. Learners will have a strong tendency to hear the sounds of English in terms of the sounds of their native language. If you've never seen a lime before you may think it is an unripe lemon because that is the nearest equivalent of the fruits you are familiar with. You may continue in your misperception until you actually eat one or until someone points out the difference to you. Sounds aren't like fruit (sound images are different from visual images), but the process of establishing categories is basically the same and each language has its own set of categories. Teachers need to check that their learners are hearing sounds according to the appropriate categories and help them to develop new categories if necessary.

Helping learners make sounds

Some sounds of English do not occur in other languages. Sometimes learners will be able to imitate the new sound, but if they can't then the teacher needs to be able to give some hints which may help them to make the new sound(s).

Providing feedback

Both the above tasks require the teacher to tell learners how they are doing. Often learners themselves can't tell if they've 'got it right'; the teacher must provide them with information about their performance. In other cases, learners may overdo something – they may make inaccurate assumptions about the way English is pronounced, perhaps because of the way it is written. This leads us to another task for the teacher:

Pointing out what's going on

Learners need to know what to pay attention to and what to work on. Because speaking is for the most part unconsciously controlled, learners may miss something important. For example, they may not realize that when a particular word is stressed or said in a different way this can affect the message that is sent to the listener. Teachers need to make learners aware of the potential of sounds – the *resources* available to them for sending spoken messages.

Establishing priorities

Learners themselves will be aware of some of the features of their pronunciation that are 'different', but they will not be able to tell if this is important or not. They may notice that something about their pronunciation is not like the way English people do it and may automatically try to change this, but their efforts are misplaced because that feature is a refinement, or acceptable to the English ear, or not essential for intelligible speech. Learners need the help of the teacher in establishing a plan for action, in deciding what to concentrate on and when to leave well enough alone.

Devising activities

Learning pronunciation is so complex that the teacher must consider what types of exercises and activities will be helpful. Which activities will provide the most opportunities for practice, experimentation, exploration? In designing activities for learning, teachers must also keep in mind that certain activities suit the learning styles and approaches of some learners better than others.

Assessing progress

This is actually a type of feedback – learners find it difficult to assess their own progress so teachers must provide the information. This is especially difficult in the elusive activity of 'making sounds', but information about progress is often a crucial factor in maintaining motivation.

1.2
The learner's role

Having listed the various aspects of the teacher's role, we could say very simply that all learners need to do is *respond*. But of course it is not as simple as that. This kind of attitude ignores the fact that ultimately success in pronunciation will depend on how much effort the learner puts into it. A major theme of Part One will be the importance of the learner's willingness to take responsibility for his or her own learning. The teacher may be highly skilled at noticing mispronunciations and pointing these out, but if learners take no action and do not try to monitor their own efforts, then the prospects of change or improvement are minimal.

1.3 Pronunciation goals

We come now to the question of what goals should be set for individual learners or groups of learners. How 'good' should the learner's pronunciation aim to be? Whereas some time ago it might have been said that the goal should always be native-like pronunciation, even though it was realized that this would be achieved by relatively few, most people now think that this is an inappropriate goal for most learners. The great majority of learners will have a very practical purpose for learning English and will derive no particular benefit from acquiring a native-like pronunciation.

There will be some learners, however, who may want to approach a native-like accent because their work requires them to deal on equal terms with native speakers in an English-speaking country or abroad. In this case, we must use criteria which are occupation-related. Learners who plan to become teachers of English will want to approximate a native accent and, depending on their future teaching situations, may want to be familiar with several of the major accents of English in the world. Learners who want to work as air traffic controllers or telephone operators, for example, will need to have a pronunciation which is easily understood in less-than-ideal conditions. In these situations there is a limited opportunity for repetition and second tries; indeed, these can be dangerous.

In many countries English has a particular role as the language of communication between people who are speakers of the different indigenous languages. The multilingual nations of India and Africa are good examples of this. These speakers of English as a second language may have a restricted audience; they will be using English only with other non-native speakers and therefore a pronunciation which is native-like is totally inappropriate. However, it must be accepted that, if there is occasion to speak with natives, the divergences in pronunciation may lead to communication breakdown.

While native-like pronunciation may be a goal for particular learners, and while we should never actively discourage learners from setting themselves 'high' goals, for the majority of learners a far more reasonable goal is to be *comfortably intelligible*. We will be looking carefully at the notion of intelligibility in the next chapter, but let us focus on the word 'comfortably'. It is significant that in English and many other languages we can make a distinction between 'hearing' and 'listening'. Hearing requires mere presence plus ears, listening requires work; we can ask someone to 'listen carefully' and accuse someone of not listening to what we have said. We all realize that some people are more difficult to listen to than others, and when we listen to a foreigner speaking our native language we expect to have to work a little bit harder. But if we have *too* hard a time – if the person pronounces in such a way that we have to constantly ask for repetitions – then at some stage we reach our threshold of tolerance. We become irritated, and maybe even resentful of the effort that is being required of us. In some cases we may be willing to be patient and ultra-tolerant, in some cases we may have to be (for example, if the speaker has some hold over us, such as a customs official at a border control), but for the most part we expect conversations with non-native speakers to be 'comfortable'. In setting goals for our learners we must consider the effect of mispronunciation on the listener and the degree of tolerance listeners will have for this.

1.4
Factors that affect pronunciation learning

The native language is an important factor in learning to pronounce English; this is clearly demonstrated by the fact that a foreign accent has some of the sound characteristics of the learner's native language. These are often obvious enough to make a person's origins identifiable by untrained as well as trained people. One or two features are enough to suggest a particular language 'showing through' their spoken English.

1.4.1
The native language

Because of the role that native language plays, there has been a great deal of research in which the sound systems of English and other languages are compared and the problems and difficulties of learners predicted. (In Part Two we will be referring to the findings of such studies.) This applies not only to the individual sounds but also to combinations of sounds and features such as rhythm and intonation. To put it very crudely, the more differences there are, the more difficulties the learner will have in pronouncing English. We can even say that there are 'more favoured' and 'less favoured' languages. But we must be careful not to over-simplify the situation and think too much in terms of handicap or barriers to learning. To do this would be to ignore what we know to be demonstrable – that people from many different language backgrounds can and do acquire a near-native pronunciation in English – and to deny the role of other factors.

1.4.2
The age factor

We commonly assume that if someone pronounces a second language like a native, they probably started learning it as a child. Conversely, if a person doesn't begin to learn a second language until adulthood, they will never have a native-like accent even though other aspects of their language such as syntax or vocabulary may be indistinguishable from those of native speakers. These beliefs seem to be supported by the many cases of adults who learn to speak a second language fluently, but still maintain a foreign accent, even when they have lived in the host country for many years. Linguists and language teachers have both been fascinated by the question: Is there an age-related limit on the mastery of pronunciation in a second language? This is a much-researched topic, but the studies have unfortunately yielded conflicting results. We will briefly summarize the findings of a few of the studies that have been carried out and survey some of the recent research on this topic.

Oyama[1] carried out a study of Italian learners of English in the USA. The subjects (sixty male Italian-born immigrants) were tape-recorded reading aloud a short paragraph and telling a story about a frightening episode in their lives (completely unprepared or rehearsed). Two expert judges listened to the samples and gave each subject a score on a five point scale, ranging from 'no foreign accent' to 'heavy foreign accent'. The analysis of the results showed that the younger a person was when he started learning English (i.e. the age of arrival in the USA) the more native-like was his accent. This study seems to show that learning to pronounce like a native is very difficult for all but the very young. As Oyama put it: '. . . really native-like pronunciation in a second language seems as rare in an adult learner as the ability to run the 4 minute mile'.[2]

Another study[3] surveyed 400 people in two countries who had begun learning English at varying ages. Briefly, the judgements made about their foreign accents showed that if learning had begun before age 11 or so accents were rare, between 11 and 15 they were not uncommon, and after 15 they were virtually universal. So, these and many other studies[4] support the hypothesis that age determines the accuracy of a learner's pronunciation.

However, other studies have reached different conclusions. Snow and Hoefnagel-Höhle (1975)[5] investigated the pronunciation of speakers of British English who were learning Dutch as a second language in Holland. Their study had two parts: first, a laboratory study in which the 136 subjects were asked to listen to five Dutch words and then try to imitate them; second, a long-term study in which the subjects were tested in much the same way at intervals during their first year of learning Dutch in a Dutch-speaking environment. The results of the laboratory study showed that the two oldest groups of learners (eight 17-year-olds and seven adults of 21 to 31 years old) received the highest scores, i.e. their pronunciation was the best. The two youngest groups scored the lowest (ten 5-year-olds and ten 6-year-olds).

In the second part of the study, forty-seven English speakers ranging in age from 3 to 60 years were tested at various times during their first year of learning Dutch in Holland in a natural setting such as school or work, without any formal instruction. In the tests the subjects had first to imitate eighty words immediately after a Dutch speaker, and then to say the same words without a model, in response to a picture cue. Results from these tests showed that older people seemed to have an initial advantage, but by four to five months after starting to learn Dutch, age differences seem to have disappeared. Near the end of the first year of learning the younger children excelled in the pronunciation of some sounds, but there was still no overall age difference.

So, according to this study, youth confers no immediate advantage in learning to pronounce foreign sounds. In the short term, older subjects were considerably better than younger subjects, and only after a period of about a year did younger children begin to excel. Another interesting observation was that, after a time, the progress of the older subjects seemed to level off, whereas the children continued to progress. After eighteen months the researchers had the opportunity to test eleven of the original subjects again. Only one of them had a truly native-like pronunciation – a teenager. Other studies have similarly concluded that age is not the crucial and only factor.

Can these conflicting results be reconciled? When trying to weigh up the evidence, we have to keep two points in mind. The first point is that different investigations have assessed pronunciation in different ways. Within this range of techniques and methods there is room for discrepancies, conflict between judges about what constitutes a 'slight accent' or a 'noticeable accent' and so on. Secondly, it is extremely difficult to control for other factors which may be involved, such as ability, attitude, motivation, or opportunity to use and hear the language. Many of these factors have been referred to by investigators in their attempts to provide explanations for the age differences they have found.

Some researchers claim that there is a sensitive period for language learning, and that biological changes take place in the brain after a certain age (usually said to be between 10 and 13 years). The claim is that people actually lose certain abilities after this age.

One recent study[6] seems to suggest that the younger a person is, the better he or she will be at accurate perception of the sounds of new languages, but that recent and/or continuous exposure to new language sounds prevents this ability from deteriorating. In this case, the age factor would actually be closely related to the fact that children have had very recent exposure to new sounds because they have just learned their first language.

The evidence is contradictory and the various interpretations and possibilities are intriguing, but one thing seems clear – we do not yet have evidence for a simple and straightforward link between age and the ability to pronounce a new language. Let's look at some of the other factors which may be involved.

1.4.3 Amount of exposure

Another factor is the amount of exposure to English the learner receives. It is tempting to view this simply as a matter of whether the learner is living in an English-speaking country or not. If this is the case, then the learner is 'surrounded' by English and this constant exposure should affect pronunciation skills. If the learner is not living in an English-speaking environment, then there is no such advantage.

But it is obvious that we cannot talk simply in terms of residency. Many learners live in an English-speaking country, but spend much of their time in a non-English-speaking environment (for example, a language other than English is used at home). Conversely, many people live in non-English-speaking countries but use English in many areas of their lives, such as work or school. In such complex bilingual and multilingual situations it is difficult to get an accurate picture of how much exposure to English a learner has received, and of what kind. In addition, it is not *merely* exposure that matters, but how the learner responds to the opportunities to listen to and use English. Various studies[7] have compared the pronunciation accuracy of people living in an English-speaking country and those who are not, and it seems that amount of exposure, though clearly a contributory factor, is not a necessary factor for the development of pronunciation skills.

1.4.4 Phonetic ability

It is a common view that some people have a 'better ear' for foreign languages than others. This skill has been variously termed 'aptitude for oral mimicry', 'phonetic coding ability' or 'auditory discrimination ability'. Researchers have designed tests which measure this ability[8] and have demonstrated that some people are able to discriminate between two sounds better than others, and/or are able to mimic sounds more accurately. But every human being, unless hearing-impaired, has this basic ability; if they did not they would not have learned the sounds of the native language. We are not talking about an all-or-nothing situation, and we know that training has an effect. Far more interesting is the question of whether certain types of learners, poor discriminators and good discriminators, benefit from different types of training. One study has indicated that those with good phonetic abilities benefit from pronunciation drills, tasks in which particular sounds are heard and the learner has to imitate again and again. Their innate abilities enable them to exploit all the opportunities to compare what they are doing with the model presented. 'Poor discriminators' do not seem to benefit from drills very much. In fact, drills seem to cause their attempts to stabilize *before* they reach an accurate production of a sound. Because of the complexities involved, this seems a factor which is very much out of the control of the teacher. We can only operate on the assumption that our learners have the 'basic equipment' and provide a variety of tasks so that something will suit the needs and abilities of each learner.

1.4.5
Attitude and identity

It has been claimed that factors such as a person's 'sense of identity' and feelings of 'group affiliation' are strong determiners of the acquisition of accurate pronunciation of a foreign language. As a means of exploring the meaning of these terms and the role of such factors, let's start by considering how native speakers of a language react to different accents of their own languages.

Suppose an Australian moves to the United States, or a Spaniard moves from Barcelona to Seville, or an American takes up residence in Great Britain. Will the Australian begin to speak with an American accent? Will the Spanish speaker lose the characteristic 'th' sound and replace it with the 's' characteristic of most other Spanish accents? Will the American begin to use different vowels in 'can' and 'can't' instead of the same vowel? It is difficult to predict whether people will modify their accent or not, and, if they do, to what extent and in what ways. Individuals seem to vary greatly. Some seem to be 'impervious' and even after a long time will absorb only some turns of phrase and the pronunciation of a few individual words; others seem very receptive and begin to change their accent almost as soon as they step off the plane!

Interestingly, analysis of people in conversation has shown that adopting and imitating the way our partner speaks is a way of showing positive and friendly feelings towards that person, a subtle way of saying, 'I am glad to be talking with you.' For example, there are two alternative pronunciations of 'either' in English – one with the vowel in 'see' and the other with the vowel in 'eye'. Someone who usually uses the former may switch to the latter if the person they are talking to uses that pronunciation. It's almost as if there is a wish to avoid calling attention to any differences that exist between two people. If the newcomer consistently gives this type of signal of solidarity to virtually everyone he or she meets in the new environment, this behaviour may very well become the source and impetus for accent change. Of course, there are other contributory factors. Age is probably important – young children seem very readily to adopt the speech style of those around them, especially their peers. Length of time spent in the new place is certainly a factor. Whether the person intends to return to the part of the country and how much the person continues to associate with people from 'back home' also seem to be important.

With these last two points, we seem to be getting nearer to a definition of the 'group affiliation' factor. If, say, the Australian never intends to return to Australia, and if the American has 'settled down for good' in the UK, it is probably more likely that they will feel close ties to the new place and that their accents will change in the direction of those around them. But if the Australian or American still feels a strong sense of identity linked to place of birth, then this may work against any change in their way of speaking. Personal commitment to a community, and a willingness to be identified with the members of that community, can be revealed through the way a person chooses to speak.

But we are concerned in this book with the pronunciation of a foreign language. Can identity and affiliation play as powerful a role here? Maybe not, but it would seem likely that the factors influencing the development of an accent in a speaker's first language also play a part in the development of an accent in a foreign language. There also seems to be some evidence for this assumption. In many studies of attitude and motivation in language learning, it has been shown that those learners who show positive feelings towards the speakers of the new language tend to develop more accurate, native-like accents. These positive feelings have been related to their 'integrative motivation'; the language learner is willing to be integrated into the new speech community and is genuinely interested both in the speakers and in their culture.[9]

1.4.6
Motivation and concern for good pronunciation

Some learners seem to be more concerned about their pronunciation than others. This concern is often expressed in statements about how 'bad' their pronunciation is and in requests for correction – both blanket requests ('Please correct my pronunciation whenever I make a mistake.') and frequent pauses during speech used to solicit comments on the accuracy of pronunciation. It may even be reflected in a reluctance to speak – the 'I don't want to say it if I can't say it perfectly' mentality. When we talk in terms of 'strength of concern' for pronunciation we are really pinpointing a type of motivation. The desire to do well is a kind of 'achievement motivation'. Conversely, if you don't care about a particular task or don't see the value of it, you won't be motivated to do well. Learners may also be unconcerned because they simply are not aware that the way they speak is resulting in difficulty, irritation or misunderstanding for the listener.

1.4.7
Conclusions

We have examined several of the factors which may affect pronunciation accuracy. The question to ask now is: 'Which of these factors can themselves be affected by teaching and training?'

Clearly, we can't change the age or the raw phonetic ability of our learners, and we can only increase exposure to a certain degree. Nor would it seem that teaching could directly affect the identity and attitudinal factors, although these may be indirectly influenced if, through their learning experiences, learners become interested in the speakers of the language and their customs and culture. However, it would seem possible to affect one of the factors we have discussed – motivation and concern for good pronunciation. We can try to do this in the following ways:

(a) We can persuade learners of the importance of good pronunciation for ease of communication.

(b) We can continually emphasize that a 'native-like' accent will not be imposed as a goal. (Intelligibility and communicative efficiency are the only realistic goals. They can be achieved as much, if not more, by the way the teacher reacts and the stance he or she adopts as by merely making statements.)

(c) We can demonstrate concern for learners' pronunciation and their progress in it.

These three points are important aspects of the teacher's role. The third is especially important. A teacher who clearly demonstrates concern for the pronunciation and speaking skills of learners will stand a good chance of instilling a similar concern in the learners themselves. A teacher who pays little or no attention to matters of pronunciation will probably induce a complacent attitude in learners ('My accent is OK'). This is fine if it is, but not if it's not!

1.5
Aspects of
pronunciation

We have talked about the teacher's role in making learners aware of pronunciation. But what are the various aspects of pronunciation? We will use one sentence to illustrate these very briefly (each aspect will be discussed in more detail in the following chapters):

There isn't any salt on the table.

First of all there are the *sounds*. These are of two types, *vowels* and *consonants*. Vowels and consonants perform different functions in the *syllable*. Each syllable has a vowel at its centre (s*a*lt, t*a*b-, etc.) and the consonants 'surround' the vowel, preceding it and cutting it off. As we see from the word 'any', it is also possible to have a syllable with just a vowel (*a*-ny).

Combinations of sounds

Sometimes sounds occur in groups. Two consonants occur at the end of the word 's*alt*'. When this happens within a word it is called a *consonant cluster*.

Linkage of sounds

When English people speak they generally do not pause between each word, but move smoothly from one word to the next. There are special ways of doing this. For example, a speaker saying our sentence will move directly from the 't' of 'sal*t*' to the 'o' of '*on*', and from the 't' of 'isn'*t*' to the 'a' of '*any*'. Demonstrate the use of linkage to yourself by saying the following three words slowly, pausing between each word:

not   at   all

Now string them together into a phrase. (Imagine someone has asked you how you liked something, and you want to tell them you didn't like it one bit.) When said in this natural way, speakers don't pause between the words, but move smoothly from the 't' sounds at the end of 'not' and 'at' to the vowel sounds at the beginning of 'at' and 'all'. In fact, when most speakers say the last word of the phrase it sounds like the word 'tall'.

Word stress

When an English word has more than one syllable (a 'polysyllabic' word) one of these is made to stand out more than the other(s). This is done by saying that syllable slightly louder, holding the vowel a little longer, and pronouncing the consonants very clearly. These features combine to give that syllable prominence or *stress*. In 'table', 'isn't', and 'any' the first syllables are stressed.

Rhythm

English speech resembles music in that it has a beat. There are groups of syllables, just like bars of music, and within each group there are strong and weaker beats. There is a tendency in English for the strong beats to fall on nouns, verbs, adjectives, and adverbs (words that carry a lot of meaning) and for the weak beats to fall on prepositions, articles, and pronouns (words with a grammatical function). If we apply this to our sentence, we get the following rhythm:

There isn't any salt on the table.

da DA da da da DA da da DA da

The following short sentence has the rhythm strong-weak-weak, strong-weak-weak:

What do you think of it?

DA da da DA da da

So, it actually has a 'waltz rhythm'.

Weak forms

When a word with only one syllable is unstressed in a sentence, its pronunciation is often quite different from when it is stressed. The definite article, 'the', is an example. When said by itself, or stressed, the vowel will sound like the one in 'me', but when it is unstressed the vowel will be quite short and indistinct. The vowel that is used in unstressed syllables most often is *schwa* /ə/. This is the name given to the vowel made with the lips and tongue in a neutral or rest position. It is the vowel sound many English people make when they hesitate during speech (it is often represented in spelling as 'uh' or 'er').

The most extreme example of a drastic change in pronunciation in our sentence is '-*n't*'. This is the unstressed form of 'not'; it has lost its vowel completely and only the two consonants remain. (These and other similar forms, such as 'I'm', 'you're', etc., are called contractions.) When a word has a special pronunciation in unstressed position this is known as its *weak form*.

10

Sentence stress

So far we've been able to say a lot about the pronunciation of our sentence just by looking at it by itself, but to go any further we must put it into a conversational context, for example:

A: There's plenty of salt.
B: There isn't any salt on the table.

Speakers often decide that they want to give more or less prominence to a particular word. A word may be given less weight because it has been said already, or it may be given more weight because the speaker wants to highlight it. In the above conversation, B would probably give extra stress to 'table', meaning: 'There may well be salt, but I want to point out to you that there isn't any in a particular place – on the table.' This aspect of pronunciation is called *sentence stress*.

Intonation

Speech is also like music in that it uses changes in pitch; speakers can change the pitch of their voice as they speak, making it higher or lower in pitch at will. They can even jump up suddenly in pitch as singers do. So speech has a melody called *intonation*. The two basic melodies are rising and falling. These can be very sudden, or gradual, and can be put together in various combinations (rise-fall-rise, fall-rise-fall, etc.).

Speakers use pitch to send various messages. For example, if A had said, 'There isn't any salt on the table', B might have repeated the same words but with gradually rising pitch and this would have had the effect of sending a message such as: 'Are you sure – I'm amazed – I was sure I put it there.' Alternatively, B might want to send the message: 'There is salt somewhere, but not on the table', in which case he could do this by using a falling then rising pitch on the word 'table'. Let's look at another example. Imagine how you would say the following if someone were about to touch a dangerous button or switch:

You mustn't touch that.

Your voice would probably start with a very high pitch and the changes in pitch would be quite extreme. In less serious circumstances, your voice pitch might be quite low and you would not use many changes in pitch. Sentence stress and intonation work together to help speakers send the precise message they want to send.

1.6
Speaking with a foreign accent

It is important to remember that the way a person speaks is a sign of their origin. Every language in the world has different varieties and different accents (these may be regional or social class accents). In some languages, there are even different styles of pronunciation for men and women. The way we speak is really a part of our identity. Much the same applies to a foreign accent; to speak English with a foreign accent amounts to a declaration: 'I am not English, I am from somewhere else.' People may actually feel (though they are not conscious of it) that there are advantages in being immediately identifiable as a foreigner, because their listeners will be aware of the possibility of misunderstanding and perhaps adjust the way they listen. It has been said that native speakers can actually be suspicious of too perfect an accent – that, in American and British cultures in particular, phoney-correctness of any kind is treated with scorn. Perhaps such feelings are akin to listeners' often negative reactions to a foreigner's use of newly-coined or slang expressions – the foreigner is seen as encroaching on private territory. A comparison has been made with a host who sees an uninvited guest making free with his possessions.[10] But if imitation is the sincerest form of flattery, then such reactions (if they do indeed exist) seem difficult to understand. Certainly the reaction of most people when they meet someone whose English is virtually indistinguishable from that of a native speaker is one of admiration and high praise.

But the most prevalent attitude held about speaking with a foreign accent is that it is the learner's 'problem'. We must try to get away from this. What we are really dealing with is a phenomenon on a level with the other accents of English – Australian accent, American accent, Scottish accent, foreign accent. Speaking with a foreign accent is only a 'problem' if it leads to a breakdown in communication.

References

1 S. Oyama 'A Sensitive Period for the Acquisition of a Nonnative Phonological System' (*Journal of Psycholinguistic Research* 5/3 1976).
2 S. Oyama p. 280.
3 S. Krashen's study quoted in Oyama.
4 See for example: Seliger, Krashen and Ladefoged 'Maturational Constraints in the Acquisition of Second Language Accent' (*Language Sciences* 36 1975) and A. Fathman 'The Relationship Between Age and Second Language Productive Ability' (*Language and Speech* 20 1977).
5 C. Snow and M. Hoefnagel-Höhle 'Age Differences in the Pronunciation of Foreign Sounds' (*Language and Speech* 20 1977).
6 J. F. Werker et al 'Developmental Aspects of Cross-language Speech Perception' (*Child Development* 52 1981).
7 See for example: E. Purcell and R. Suter 'Predictors of Pronunciation Accuracy' (*Language Learning* 30/2 1980).
8 See tests referred to in B. Helmke and Wu Yi So 'Individual Differences and Foreign Language Pronunciation Achievement' (*Revue de Phonétique Appliquée* 53 1980).
9 See for example: R. C. Gardner and W. E. Lambert *Attitudes and Motivation in Second Language Learning* (Newbury House 1972).
10 P. Christopherson *Second Language Learning: Myth and Reality* (Penguin 1973).

2

Intelligibility

Very few teachers today would claim that a pronunciation that is indistinguishable from that of a native speaker is necessary or even desirable for their learners. Instead, it is generally accepted that intelligibility is the most sensible goal. But what is meant by intelligibility? Here is one definition: 'Intelligibility is being understood by a listener at a given time in a given situation'. So, it's the same as 'understandability'. Substituting one word for another usually doesn't get one very far, let's try for a more operational definition, one that we can 'put to work': 'The more words a listener is able to identify accurately when said by a particular speaker, the more intelligible that speaker is.' Since words are made up of sounds, it seems that what we are talking about is the issue of equivalence of sounds. If the foreign speaker substitutes one sound or feature of pronunciation for another, and the result is that the listener hears a different word or phrase from the one the speaker was aiming to say, we say that the foreigner's speech is unintelligible. Likewise, if the foreign speaker substitutes a sound in a particular word, but that word is nonetheless understood, then we say the speech is intelligible.

When we set intelligibility as our goal, rather than native-like pronunciation, in practical terms this means we are aiming for something 'close enough'. In other words, although the foreign speaker doesn't make precisely the same sound or use the exact feature of linkage or stress, it is possible for the listener to match the sound heard with the sound (or feature) a native speaker would use without too much difficulty. So, what matters is 'counts of sameness'. We can compare this process with the way English-speaking adults listen and understand the speech of their young children who are learning English as their mother tongue. A child of three or four may have problems pronouncing the /r/ sound, as in '*r*un', and may use a /w/-like sound as in '*w*in'. The child may say: 'I see a wabbit'. The parents will understand that the child has seen a furry animal with long ears, because they know that /w/ *counts as* /r/ for their child. Now let's look at an example from non-native speech. Many German speakers of English substitute /v/ as in

13

'*van*' for /w/ as in '*w*ill'. Listeners who are well-used to this will have few problems understanding utterances such as 'I *v*ant to ask you' or 'I *v*ill tell you tomorrow'. They 'know' the speaker's /v/ counts as /w/.

2.1.1
Factors affecting intelligibility

We have said that intelligibility is dependent on 'counts of sameness', but other aspects of speech can affect a person's intelligibility. If, for example, a learner's speech is full of self-corrections, hesitations, and grammatical restructurings, then listeners will tend to find what he or she says difficult to follow. Here's an example:

My parents . . . has . . . I has . . . have . . . four elder sisters.[1]

Interestingly, it has been found that speakers who hesitate a lot also tend to have many pronunciation problems. There may well be a link between lack of confidence about pronunciation and pauses and hesitations, which in turn make the person difficult to understand.

Another speaker factor which is often mentioned is that the person speaks too quickly. When we have difficulty understanding a non-native speaker, we sometimes feel that if they 'just slowed down a bit' it would be easier to understand them. But it seems that speed of speech is not a vital factor in intelligibility. The speed of two speakers may be found to be the same (based on a count of syllables per second) but one will be judged to be less intelligible than the other.[2] More often than not, when we feel a speaker is speaking too fast, it's not the speed that is causing difficulties, but the fact that we can't seem to pick out the most important bits – the crucial words – from the less important bits. Look at this sentence:

We **need** to **buy** some **paint**.

Now if you were listening to someone, and you could only make out the three words in bold type, and couldn't make out the words in ordinary type, you would still 'get the message'. If it's easy for listeners to hear the 'important words', then there will probably be few intelligibility problems. Features like word and sentence stress, rhythm, and intonation are very important in highlighting the important bits of a message.

Idiosyncratic speech habits may also affect intelligibility. For example, some Chinese learners of English may use a kind of tag word at the end of each phrase, a carry-over from conversational Chinese. It sounds like 'la' and is roughly equivalent to the way English speakers interpolate OK? into their speech, but this unusual sound can confuse a native listener, who may think it is an English word.

We have discussed briefly some examples of how features of non-native speech can affect intelligibility, but we must not make the mistake of focusing too much on what our non-native speakers are doing, what we might call 'speaker factors'. Intelligibility presupposes participants. In other words, intelligibility has as much to do with the listener as with the speaker. There are two 'listener factors' which are very important: first, the listener's familiarity with the foreign accent and, second, the listener's ability to use contextual clues when listening.

Familiarity and exposure affect a person's ability to understand a particular type of accent. Let's take an example of an American speaker living in Hawaii who gets many opportunities to talk with Japanese speakers of English, but very few opportunities to hear Indian English. Various studies have shown that he or she will find an Indian speaker of English more difficult to understand than a Japanese speaker. In general, people find listening to the English of their fellow countrymen easiest, so a French speaker of English will find other French speakers of English easier to understand than, say, the English of Spanish speakers. The most obvious reason for this is that the French speakers will share features of pronunciation. It is also very likely that they have had more opportunity to listen to other French speakers speaking English. The more opportunities you have to listen to a particular type of English, the more easily intelligible that accent is to you.

This factor of familiarity and exposure works at the individual level as well. If you know a foreign speaker personally, then you will probably be able to understand him or her better than a stranger who speaks with the same type of accent.[3] To return to our comparison with the speech of young English children, it is often the case that the parents will be able to understand their child very easily, but that other adults will have problems. We can also make a comparison with the various regional accents of English – a Cockney and a Scot from Glasgow may have a great deal of trouble understanding each other, until they get used to each others' accents.

The second listener factor is the skilful way in which listeners can use clues from the other parts of the sentence to figure out a particular word. Here's an excerpt from non-native speech:

In 1983 the boys and girls get together in one corps but er mostly there are girl troops or scouts and boy scouts.

The word 'corps' was pronounced like 'car', but because words like 'scouts' and 'troop' and 'patrol' had been used many times by the speaker, the listener knew that the topic of conversation was 'the Scout movement' and was able to figure out that the word intended was 'corps'. If the topic of conversation is clear and there are plenty of meaning clues, then listeners may be able to understand a word which would have thrown them completely if it had been pronounced in isolation.

2.1.2
Intelligibility and communication

So far, we have been looking at some of the features which determine intelligibility, but it is very important to remember that the wider context of this discussion is *communication*. Foreign speakers need to be intelligible so that they can communicate. Communication involves more than simply sending a set of well-produced sounds into the air at your listener(s). It is much more complex than a radio receiver/radio transmitter model. There is first of all the question of a speaker's *intentions*. Look at this short extract from a conversation (A has been telling B a story when suddenly B bursts into laughter):

A: What are you laughing at?
B: (*stops laughing*) Oh . . . sorry.

A: No, I didn't mean you shouldn't laugh . . . I really want to know what you found funny.

B thought A's question was intended as a command to stop laughing, as a criticism (perhaps because of their relationship or A's facial expression). But it was simply a straightforward information question. So, although B understood every word A said, B misunderstood what A intended by those words. Communication involves reading the other's intentions. Determining what the other speaker intended can be tricky. Ultimately we can only guess intentions – they actually only exist in the other person's mind. But listeners must try to get it right, so they use all the information available to them to guess intentions. This may include what one knows about the speaker, about the situation, about what has just been said and so on. When there is a great deal of this type of information available, the listener's task is easier.

There is also the question of *effective* communication. Imagine this situation: you are in a room full of seated people – let's say a cinema; suddenly someone stands up and shouts a word or words that no one understands; the person is obviously very agitated, and is pointing towards an open door; smoke and the smell of something burning waft through the door; everyone immediately makes for the fire exits. The attempt at communication has obviously been *effective* even though the word was not intelligible. This is an extreme example of using clues from the context to guess a speaker's intentions.

Finally there is the question of *efficiency*. A person may eventually understand what someone has said, but if this has involved too much frustration and irritation resulting from constant repetitions, rephrasings, or checks on what has been said (i.e. 'too much pain') then the communication cannot be described as efficient. The chances are very high that neither party will be eager to repeat the experience. As we have said before, the pronunciation goal must be *comfortable intelligibility*.

Clearly the issue of intelligibility is very complex and the notions of efficiency, effectiveness, and speaker's intentions are crucial issues. To the teacher who wants an answer to the question: 'How can I ensure that the sounds my learners make will be counted as the same as those of native speakers?' these may seem like side issues, but they are not. Teachers must keep these points in mind, or run the risk of 'getting it wrong' by operating with too narrow a view of what needs to be done to improve intelligibility and by looking for easy answers.

In this introductory section we have looked briefly at the notion of intelligibility and how central it is in matters of pronunciation. In the next section we will examine the sources of *un*intelligibility in detail.

2.2 Sources of intelligibility problems

In coping with a new set of sounds, learners use a variety of strategies. Perhaps the most basic of these is a strategy which might be stated as: 'I can use the sounds of my own language to speak English.' Other strategies might involve trying to avoid certain sounds (although this is a very difficult one to put into practice!). Of course, these are not conscious strategies. Nor are the results of coping strategies always negative. Some ways of coping may lead to success; others will lead to problems. Let's look at some examples of learner pronunciation strategies which can lead to intelligibility problems.

2.2.1
Sound substitutions

We've already seen an example of a vowel substitution problem. The learner who substituted the vowel /ɑ/ as in 'p*art*' for /ɔ/ ('c*aw*') when saying the word 'corps' created a potential source of unintelligibility. So, if a speaker substitutes one sound for another, this may cause difficulties for the listener. Some sound substitutions are not very serious and the chances that the word will be correctly identified by the listener are good, because the substituted sound is 'close enough' to count as 'the same' to the listener. But in some instances the learner may substitute a sound which also happens to be a significant sound in English, 'a sound in its own right'. For example, many speakers whose native languages do not have the 'th' sound as in '*th*ick' will substitute the sound /s/ as in 'sick' for it. But /s/ is also a significant sound of English, so, in a sense, one sound has collided and fused with another in the learner's speech. The two words 'sick' and 'thick' will be pronounced exactly the same. Unless context helps the listener, or this feature of non-native speech is familiar, the listener will have to decide whether the speaker said 'My friend is sick' or 'My friend is thick' (i.e. stupid).

2.2.2
Sound deletions

Another set of problems might be given the cover term 'deletion', where the speaker leaves out a sound. In the case of consonants, a single consonant at the beginning, middle, or end of a word may be deleted, or one or two of the consonants in a group or cluster may be deleted. An example would be the word 'hold' pronounced without the final 'd' – it would sound like 'hole'.

2.2.3
Sound insertions

Non-native speakers may add sounds. For example, many learners when pronouncing words like 'speak', 'spoon' or 'Spain' add a short vowel sound at the beginning of these words. So 'speak' may sound like 'a-speak', a two-syllable word.

2.2.4
Links between words

All the above problems concern sounds within a word, but there may also be problems at the borders of words. In English, word boundaries are 'negotiated' in certain ways: sometimes a linking sound is used, sometimes one sound merges with another, and sometimes a composite sound is used. Here are examples of each of these types of links:

a linking sound
When saying 'go in', speakers add the consonant /w/ as in '*w*ill'. It sounds like 'go win'. When saying 'the aim . . .' English speakers will insert the consonant /j/ as in 'yes' between the two words. It sounds something like 'the yame'.

a sound merger
When saying 'nice shoe' the final consonant of 'nice' merges with the first consonant of 'shoe'. The result sounds like 'ny shoe'.

a composite sound

When saying 'this year' English speakers may use the consonant /ʃ/ as in '*sh*oe' at the border between the two words. They will not pronounce the 's' followed by /j/ as in 'yes' but use this 'composite' sound. The phrase will sound quite like 'the shear'.

We have already mentioned that speakers normally move smoothly from the final sound of one word to the initial sound of the next word (see the 'not at all' example in 1.5). If learners do not use these typical English features, or, even more crucially, if they use very different ways of linking words, then it can be very difficult for English listeners to identify the phrases in an utterance – the words that belong together. Chinese learners often do not use smooth transitions; this can make their speech sound very staccato and jerky. Other speakers tend to insert short sounds between words. For example, an Italian learner might say the following:

It's a big-a one (for 'It's a big one').

These un-English ways of linking words make life very difficult for the English listener. In the above example, the listener may try to attach the extra sound to words already identified and might come up with:

It's a bigger one.

When confronted by poor linkage, listeners may have the feeling that they are 'lost' in the stream of speech.

2.2.5
The use of stress

In English there is a special relationship between the different parts of a word. As we have seen in 1.5, in an English word of two or more syllables, one of these will have 'prominence' or 'stress'. That syllable is perceived as more prominent because of a complex of features such as loudness, length of vowel, etc. If the learner doesn't stress one syllable more than another, or stresses the wrong syllable, it may be very difficult for the listener to identify the word. This is because the stress pattern of a word is an important part of its identity for the native speaker. There is a great deal of evidence that native speakers rely very much on the stress pattern of words when they are listening. In fact, experiments have demonstrated that often when a native speaker mishears a word, it is because the foreigner has put the stress in the wrong place, not because he or she mispronounced the sounds of the word. Here are some examples:[4]

– the word 'written' was pronounced with the stress on the second syllable instead of on the first. The listener thought the speaker had said 'retain'.

– 'comfortable' was pronounced with stress on 'com-' and on '-ta-'. The listener heard this as 'come for a table'.

– 'productivity', which has the pattern pro duc <u>tiv</u> i ty, was pronounced with a stress on '-duc-' and one on '-ty' (pro <u>duc</u> tiv i <u>ty</u>). This was heard as 'productive tea' (and caused considerable confusion!).

In all the above cases, the sounds used by the speaker were for the most part accurate. But despite this, the listeners were thrown by the incorrect stress pattern. If we examine each of the examples, we see that, in all cases, what the listener thought he or she heard has exactly the same stress pattern as the one the speaker actually used. In the first example, the speaker said writ<u>ten</u> and the listener heard re<u>tain</u>. Many other cases of misunderstanding reveal upon analysis that the listener is paying as much attention to stress pattern as to the individual sounds.

2.2.6
The use of rhythm

English has a characteristic rhythm and listeners *expect* to hear all speakers use this rhythm. It is therefore absolutely vital that learners use the rhythm that is characteristic of English. There must be an alternation of stressed and unstressed syllables, with the stressed syllables occurring on a regular beat, and the unstressed syllables must have a less-than-full vowel. Demonstrate this to yourself by saying the following two statements out loud:

I'm <u>twenty</u>-<u>one</u> to<u>mor</u>row.   I'm <u>seventy</u>-<u>seven</u> to<u>mor</u>row.

Notice that the stressed (underlined) syllables occur at regular intervals in time. Although the first sentence has seven syllables and the second has nine, they both have the same rhythm, three stressed syllables (or four if you stress 'I'm'), and they both take about the same amount of time to say. This is because the unstressed syllables, no matter how many there are, are 'squeezed' in between the strong stresses, so that the regular beat of the stressed syllables is not disturbed. Only the stressed syllables have a full vowel. The first unstressed syllable of 'tomorrow' has the schwa vowel (it is *not* pronounced the same as the word 'two'), as does the second syllable of 'seven'. The syllable '-ty' has a very short vowel (compare it with its full version in 'I'd like some *tea*').

If the speaker doesn't use the characteristic English rhythm, then the listener will be placed in the position of someone who walks out onto the dance floor with a partner, expecting to waltz, but finds that the partner starts some strange set of syncopated steps which are thoroughly unpredictable and impossible to follow, or marches up and down in a perfectly steady beat, which doesn't seem like dancing at all to the waltz-lover!

2.2.7
The use of intonation

Finally there is the matter of pitch variation and 'tunes' in English. Listeners get certain information from the pitch of the voice and speakers send information using pitch variation. Intonation is important for intelligibility, because it is used to express intentions. A speaker can show that he or she is asking for information, or asking for confirmation, seeking agreement, or simply making a remark that is indisputable or 'common knowledge', through the intonation of the voice. Even though pitch rarely causes problems with the identification of words, an inappropriate intonation pattern can lead to misunderstanding just as a mispronounced sound can. Only those who take an extremely narrow view of intelligibility can disregard the importance of intonation. Furthermore, the effect of intonation can be *cumulative*; the misunderstandings may be minor, but if they occur constantly then they may result in judgements about the attitudes, character, ways of behaving, etc. of a particular speaker. For example, if a foreign speaker always uses very low pitch, without much variation in the melody of the voice, listeners may get the impression that they are 'bored' or 'uninterested' when this is really not the case.

These are the differences and deviations that can lead to intelligibility problems. Which of these occur will to a large extent be determined by the native language. For example, French and Turkish have a very different rhythm from English. If a French speaker is difficult to understand, this may be because he or she has used a 'transfer' strategy and is using French rhythmic features when speaking English. Chinese speakers tend to have problems at the edges of words; they have difficulty linking words together and pronouncing consonants in groups and their principal coping strategy is to delete sounds.

2.3 Assessing intelligibility

The easiest way to assess the intelligibility of particular speakers is simply to ask someone to listen to them speak and say how difficult or easy they are to understand. Such impressionistic or 'subjective' assessments are both accurate and dependable. There have been several studies in which both subjective and other 'objective' assessments (based on carefully designed procedures and statistical analysis) have been carried out on the same speakers. The results of the two types of assessment tend to agree.[5] Listeners are also able to rank a group of speakers in order of intelligibility and these impressionistic rankings also tend to agree with the results of other objective ranking techniques.

So the good news is that one doesn't need complicated tests and procedures to assess the intelligibility of non-native speakers. One simply needs someone to listen to their speech. But the not-so-good news is that teachers themselves are unsuitable as judges of intelligibility. This is because of the factors of exposure and familiarity discussed in 2.1.1. By talking to someone you become accustomed to their voice. It is often the case that when you first meet someone, you may find them quite difficult to understand, but in very little time you find you have no difficulty at all in understanding their speech. Your contact with them has enabled you to tune in to their accent. Their way of speaking has not changed, but your way of listening has. A teacher is therefore a poor judge of the intelligibility of his or her own students simply because of this familiarity factor. Furthermore, teachers also get a great deal of exposure to non-native accents. Because of this constant exposure, teachers develop special skills as listeners, but these skills make them atypical listeners and therefore unsuitable as judges of intelligibility.[6] If a teacher finds a particular learner difficult to understand, then it is very likely that 'normal' listeners will find that person virtually unintelligible, at least on some occasions. It follows from this, that teachers should not be used as judges of improvement in pronunciation; what may be assessed as better pronunciation may actually be better listening on the part of the teacher.

The ideal judges are listeners who have not had an abnormal amount of exposure to non-native speech nor any previous contact with the speakers being assessed. These may be difficult to find in certain situations, but judgements by teachers of English are of limited value.

Non-native listeners can also be used as judges. The best source of this type of judge is, of course, other learners of English in the class or school. Their assessments of intelligibility are also of limited use, in that they will only tell us how difficult it is for *other* non-native speakers to understand a particular speaker. However, many learners of English may use it to communicate predominantly, or at least some of the time, with other non-native speakers, and some learners may know that their future use of English will be exclusively with other non-native speakers, so these assessments can be useful and relevant.

In the next section we will look at ways of assessing intelligibility, and ways of identifying the sources of problems.

2.3.1
Ways of analysing ease of intelligibility

Let's say a teacher has a new class of intermediate learners and wants an indication of each learner's intelligibility. We will discuss three ways of getting this information. All of them require a sample of the learners' speech.

The sample

What kind of sample is best – reading aloud or spontaneous speech? Reading aloud is a task that makes many learners very anxious; it's not something many people have to do very often. Moreover, studies have shown that learners tend to make more pronunciation errors when reading aloud than when speaking spontaneously, because the written forms of words may induce 'spelling pronunciations' or spelling interference, especially in words which have cognates in the learner's native language.[7] A sample of spontaneous speech is preferable to a read-aloud sample, mainly because this is what learners will be doing in the outside world (unless they intend to be newsreaders!).

But there are problems with spontaneous speech. If learners are told to 'speak on a topic' some may talk quite happily, but others may feel self-conscious and be very hesitant, not saying much at all. At least with a reading-aloud task, roughly equivalent stretches of speech are being judged. On balance, it's probably best to go for a spontaneous speech sample, with a bit of reading aloud, mainly to provide the teacher with information on potential spelling interference problems.

The topic of the sample

Because of the role that context or topic plays in listening, it is important that the samples of speech are on the same topic, but not identical. If the learners are all asked to read the same passage aloud, then by the time the judges have listened to the tenth reading, they will probably know the passage by heart. Even if learners are asked to read successive paragraphs from the same passage, the listener has more contextual clues for the later readings than for the earlier ones. But if the samples are all of learners giving a physical description of someone they know, or talking about past work experience, then they should be roughly comparable in terms of vocabulary, structure, etc. without being identical. The judges can be said to have the same kind of preparedness when listening to each sample.

21

Getting a tape-recorded sample

If there is a large number of learners who need to be assessed, or if the judges are not on the spot, then it will be necessary to make tape-recorded samples. Learners may be put off by the presence of a tape recorder and balk when asked to speak into the microphone. The teacher must try to reduce this anxiety as much as possible, and the best way to do it is to give learners a clear purpose for speaking. For example, they may be asked to describe one of a set of similar photographs, having been told that the person who listens to the tape will have to decide which photograph they are describing. Or they can be asked to describe the arrangement of objects on a table or tray, having been told that the listener will have to recreate the arrangement.[8] Using this approach it is even possible to give learners a purpose for reading aloud. Suppose the learner is asked to read aloud a set of sentences and told that each of these is the caption for a set of illustrations or photographs the listener will have; the listener's task will be to decide which caption fits which picture.

The judges

The judges can be the class teacher (if absolutely necessary), another teacher, or (ideally) an 'ordinary' listener-volunteer. The judges will either be recruited into the classroom to listen to the learners, or asked to listen to the tape recordings. Let's look first at the use of tape recordings.

Presenting a tape-recorded sample

One listener can cope with listening to about twenty minutes of speech, or ten two-minute sequences, at one sitting. Judges will need a short break between such sessions. Give the judges some sort of scoring system. A scale of 5–10 points glossed as very difficult, quite difficult, easy, very easy, etc. is workable, or you can ask them to give an indication of what percentage of the speech they understood. After the judges have allocated scores, they can also be asked to rank the speakers in order of difficulty. This is best done for groups of no more than five speakers at a time, so you may have to pause and give the judges a chance to do this, and then carry on with the next group.

Interpreting the scores

The judges' scores should be quite easy to interpret. The extremes should be obvious, those who are virtually unintelligible and those whose speech presents few difficulties. It is the identification of the first category which is crucial.

A simple classroom procedure

If neither facilities nor time are available for preparing tape recordings, then here is a way to assess ease of intelligibility in the classroom. The learners are asked to do one of the tasks mentioned above in 'getting a tape-recorded sample', or to read a short passage aloud. The judges are brought into the classroom for the few minutes it takes to do this, and give their impressions. If it is a new class, then the class teacher can be used, or another teacher or ordinary listener can be recruited. Alternatively, the learners can be set one of the speaking tasks to do in pairs; the judge circulates and gains an impression of the intelligibility of each learner. It may be necessary to organize a series of tasks or a round-robin procedure to make sure that the talk goes on long enough for the judge to hear everyone.

2.3.2
Determining the sources of unintelligibility

The techniques we have discussed so far can be used to give the teacher an idea of the ease of intelligibility; they do not help the teacher to identify *which* features of the learner's speech cause problems. For this we need techniques that allow for close analysis.

Some researchers[9] have tried to pinpoint sources of unintelligibility by playing a sample of speech to judges and asking them to press a buzzer or switch when they didn't understand something. The investigator would go back and analyse what the learner had said just before the buzzer was pressed. But it was found that this didn't work because, first, listeners were not very consistent about how often and when they pressed the buzzer; and, second, when a listener doesn't understand something, he or she usually waits and tries to collect some clues. We are all familiar with the feeling that we haven't understood something and then, suddenly, it 'clicks'.

The researchers who have tackled this problem have concluded that the most useful information about the sources of unintelligibility can be collected by asking the judges to listen to a short phrase or clause and then to repeat aloud, or immediately write down, what they heard. These repetitions are then compared with the original. For example, in one study[10] the listeners heard a speaker read the following:

The North wind admitted that the sun was stronger.

One listener wrote:

After the meeting, the sound was stronger.

By comparing these sentences, we can surmise that something is wrong with the student's vowels, in particular the /ɪ/ vowel ('-m*i*t-') and the /ʌ/ vowel ('s*u*n').

The write-down-what-you-hear version (from a tape recording) allows the most time for analysis. The procedure is described below.

Preparing material

Because there is a limit to what a listener can remember, the chunks of speech have to be controlled for length. Each should be between ten to fifteen words in length and have only slightly more syllables, perhaps twelve to seventeen. The average length should be about ten words/thirteen syllables. Short stretches of speech of this length can be taken out of longer stretches, but it is probably easier to use one of the methods described in 2.3.1 to get the sample. The chunks of speech should be on everyday topics, but it may be useful to include a few unusual topics that are not 'common knowledge' to check whether the speaker is likely to be intelligible in situations where there are few contextual clues to help the listener. (The 'North wind' example was one of this type.)

Presenting the material to judges

The judges listen to each chunk and write down what they hear. There should be a twenty second pause to allow time for this, and this time allowance should be adhered to. (Judges shouldn't have a lot more time for one stretch than for another.) Again, if tape-recording facilities are not available, a live-dictation format can be used.

You will hear ＿＿ different speakers say some short sentences. Give them a score from 1–5 depending on **how easy** you find them to understand.
1 = very easy   5 = very difficult

	1	2	3	4	5
Speaker 1					
Speaker 2					
Speaker 3					
Speaker 4					
Speaker 5					

You will hear ＿＿ sentences. Write down exactly what you hear.

S1＿＿＿＿＿＿＿＿＿＿＿

S2＿＿＿＿＿＿＿＿＿＿＿

S3＿＿＿＿＿＿＿＿＿＿＿

S4＿＿＿＿＿＿＿＿＿＿＿

S5＿＿＿＿＿＿＿＿＿＿＿

Two sample score sheets

Analysing the results

By comparing the speaker's production with the judge's version, it is possible to pinpoint sources of problems and derive from them the priorities of the teaching programme. For instance, it was this type of analysis that indicated that word stress placement was crucial for intelligibility, as discussed above in 2.2.5.

A scoring system can also be used to give an overall picture of the learner's pronunciation. Any deviation in the written version is given a minus point. Each missing word scores a minus point (listeners often draw a blank line when they can't make out a word at all) as well as each incorrect word. The more minuses, the more *un*intelligible the learner is. So this technique can be used to give an assessment of ease of intelligibility too.

But what if the listener produces a paraphrase, without word-for-word accuracy? Our scoring method should take this into account, because it may be a listener or task-related factor rather than a learner factor. One way to do this is to award points for 'thought groups'. For example, if the speaker said:

so I went to a free school

there are seven words and two thought groups; one, somebody went somewhere and two, that place was a free school. If the listener wrote:

so I went to Frisco

the score could be 4 out of 7 for words correct, and 1 out of 2 for thought groups. This speaker could be given two numerical scores, which could also be expressed as a percentage of possible correct items, in this case 70 per cent and 50 per cent.[11]

2.3.3
Concluding
remarks

All the techniques discussed in this section require analysis and preparation time. Also, if the teacher is familiar with the types of problems particular groups of learners tend to have (i.e. the type of information provided in Part Two) then the speech samples can be checked against the 'list' and an appropriate teaching programme devised. Teachers must decide how much time and resources are available for these kinds of activities. But their usefulness is not simply diagnostic, they provide an excellent way to assess progress in pronunciation. After a period of time, more samples can be made of the learners' speech. These later samples are mixed with the earlier samples and assessed or analysed in the ways described above. If there has been progress in the area of pronunciation, the scores for the later samples should be better than the scores for the earlier samples. These techniques also provide ways to involve learners in self-analysis and evaluation. These applications will be explored in detail in Chapter 6, but we will mention one advantage of exploiting them here.

Individual learners may arrive with a false estimate of their intelligibility. This may be because they have previously spoken English only with their fellow countrymen or with others who were familiar with their accent. They may need to be made aware that they cause problems for other listeners, for example, strangers or native speakers. Doing a dictation task or one of the tape-recording activities outlined above may persuade the learner that improvement in pronunciation is needed when the teacher's remarks have had no effect. Conversely, such tasks may ease the anxiety of a learner who is overly self-conscious about pronunciation and need not be. These tasks can be used as part of the process of making learners aware and concerned about their pronunciation. This process is the subject of the next chapter.

References

1 Example quoted from D. Albrechsten et al 'Native Speaker Reactions to Learner's Spoken Interlanguage' (*Language Learning* 30/2 1980).
2 R. K. Bansal *The Intelligibility of Indian English* (Hyderabad 1969).
3 S. Gass and E. Varonis 'The Effect of Familiarity on the Comprehensibility of Non-native Speech' (*Language Learning* 34/1 1984).
4 I am grateful to Mr V. Mahandra, London Borough of Newham, for the second and third examples, and to Bansal (1969) for the first.
5 L. Smith and J. Bisazza 'The Comprehensibility of Three Varieties of English for College Students in Seven Countries' (*Language Learning* 32/2 1982).
6 Gass and Varonis (1984).
7 H. Hammerley 'Contrastive Phonology and Error Analysis' (*International Review of Applied Linguistics* xx/1 1982).

8 G. Brown and G. Yule *Teaching the Spoken Language* (Cambridge University Press 1983).
9 R. K. Bansal (1969).
10 Gass and Varonis (1984).
11 This technique has been adapted from D. Brodkey 'Dictation as a Measure of Intelligibility' (*Language Learning* 22/2 1972).

3

Building awareness and concern for pronunciation

Learning to pronounce a language is a very complex task and, as with any other complex learning task, the learning process can be facilitated if the task is structured in some way and if the learner is aware of exactly what is involved. It is difficult for learners to do this for themselves, so it is the teacher's job. This means dividing the task into its components, ordering the components in some way (for instance, from basic to complex, or easy to difficult) and showing the learner why each component must be learnt. For example, one component of tennis is learning how to serve. Serving can be divided into: (1) how to hold the racket; (2) tossing up the ball; (3) striking the ball; (4) placing the ball; (5) varying the speed and direction of the ball, and so on. The novice must realize that it is vital to toss the ball up well; if he doesn't, then he won't be able to hit it at the correct angle to produce an effective serve. Similarly, English pronunciation has various components such as sounds, stress, and variation in pitch, and the learner needs to understand the function of these as well as their form.

Once learners are aware that English words have a stress pattern, that words can be pronounced in slightly different ways, that the pitch of the voice can be used to convey meaning, then they will know *what* to pay attention to and can build upon this basic awareness.

Learners also need to develop a *concern* for pronunciation. They must recognize that poor, unintelligible speech will make their attempts at conversing frustrating and unpleasant both for themselves and for their listeners. They must also realize that success in language learning, as in any learning task, involves setting oneself goals, and working hard to achieve them.

The activities described in this chapter should be viewed as a first stage in the learning process – a way to 'open the ears' and establish strategies and methods of working which can later be consolidated and extended.

We will begin by looking at activities for introducing learners to all the components of English pronunciation, and then at some ways of persuading learners that 'pronunciation is important' – general awareness-building activities.

3.1
Word stress

Correct word stress patterns are essential for the learner's production and perception of English. If a non-native speaker produces a word with the wrong stress pattern, an English listener may have great difficulty in understanding the word, even if most of the individual sounds have been well pronounced. In listening, if learners of English expect a word to have a particular stress pattern, they may not recognize it when a native speaker says it. In other words, what they hear doesn't match what they have in their mental dictionary.

3.1.1
Using names

Here are some ways of making learners aware of word stress patterns in English. The first set of activities focuses on the pronunciation of proper names and place names. Because of the restriction in the vocabulary corpus, these activities are suitable for the lower levels of proficiency. The second set of activities involves more vocabulary and writing and reading skills, and is appropriate for the higher levels of proficiency (intermediate and post-intermediate).

Names of class members[1]

The teacher can demonstrate the importance of stress pattern in the English language by showing concern for the correct pronunciation of the names of members of the class. (This activity can be done in the very first lesson, indeed in the first minutes with a new class. How better to draw attention to this aspect of English?)

Procedure
Ask each student his or her name, or call out the names from the class list. (For polysyllabic names, make a stab at the stress placement if you don't know it already.) Using rising intonation in your voice and a questioning facial expression, show that you are checking the names. When the student has identified himself or herself, show your concern for accuracy by shifting the stress to the wrong syllable. Say 'not . . .' and shake your head to show you think that pronunciation is wrong, then shift it back again to the correct syllable. So for each student's name, you will be doing something like this:

T: Carlos Domecq?
C: *raises hand or nods*
T: Not Carlos, but Carlos?
C: Carlos.
T: Carlos. (*repeating student's pronunciation*)

You may use an accompanying hand gesture to beat out the stress pattern. When you give your own name to the students, go through much the same process. If a student has a name which has an English version, you can bring this in, contrasting the English version's stress pattern with the stress pattern of the native version. For example, Mary versus Marie.

Place names and names of well-known people

Procedure

Ask the students for the names of their countries, large cities, or the names of famous people or well-known landmarks. Various means can be used to elicit a response, such as simple questions, picture cues, and maps. As each item is named, establish the stress pattern as above, shifting the stress to the wrong syllable and then back again to the correct one. At this point you may introduce a term for this phenomenon. In the early stages of work on word stress, the adjective 'loud' can be used ('Which part of the word is loudest?') 'Stress' or 'stressed' can be reserved for later stages.

Notation

A notation is also useful. Below are some of the ways that stressed syllables have been marked in books and teaching materials:

(a) LONdon

(b) 'London

(c) Lóndon

(d) London

(e) London

(a) is not very suitable for learners who are not used to the Roman alphabet and therefore for whom upper and lower case may not be very noticeable. (b) is a very quick addition to the written presentation of a word, but dictionaries vary in their use of a similar mark; some put it before the stressed syllable, some put it after, so this may be a source of confusion. (c) avoids this problem, but care needs to be taken in syllables with two vowel letters because in other languages a marking such as Éaling would show that each vowel was pronounced as a separate syllable. (d) is also quickly added to written words but like (a) it requires a decision as to syllable boundaries. (e) is quick to write and it also has the advantage that it can stand on its own to illustrate a stress pattern, as in 'O o', so it is useful in purely oral work. (b) can also be used in this way by adding a horizontal mark '_' for unstress, but a sequence of these seems more difficult to read than large and small circles or squares. Compare '__'_'__'_ with OooOoOooOo. In the early stages of working on word stress you may want to avoid written forms. Notation (e) is ideal for this. Or you could use an alternative visual mode of representation. Cuisenaire rods are one possibility – a long rod represents stress, shorter ones represent unstress. Small and large blocks can also be used, or plastic discs.[2] If there is a magnet board or felt board in the classroom, then a visual representation of stress pattern can be presented with great ease and modified just as easily by moving the circles or discs around.

Follow-up activities

The proper names or place names that you have collected can be used in any of a number of activities ranging from the practice of short question/ answer sequences to a game activity. Alternatively, you can continue the focus on pronunciation with a follow-up activity which contrasts the correct native pronunciation of place names with the incorrect non-native pronunciation. For this activity you can prepare a tape of an English speaker using short phrases in which there is a preselected set of non-English names. The learners must listen to the tape, note the stress placement the speaker uses, and compare it with the correct stress pattern. Of course, the tape-recorded voice doesn't need to get it wrong all the time; in fact, it is preferable if some of the pronunciations are correct, to keep the students on their toes. The tape analysis can be done as a class, in pairs, or in groups.

Another simple follow-up phase involves the learners in making a random collection of words: from their coursebook, from items in a wall chart or picture, by asking a volunteer to reveal the contents of a bag, and so on. Then the learners, using the teacher as informant, determine the stress pattern of each word. A simple writing task can be added by preparing a worksheet with columns, each headed by a particular pattern. Learners have to enter words in the correct column, like this:

(the contents of _____ 's handbag)

O o	o O	O o o
hairbrush	receipts	handkerchief
wallet	cassettes	eyeliner
lighter		aspirin

If the word collection contains mostly nouns of two syllables, then the O o pattern will predominate because this is the most common pattern in English. It may be wise to double-check to make sure the learners will encounter a wide selection of patterns. However, it may also be a good idea to let the O o pattern predominate and point out that this is the most likely pattern for any new two-syllable word. This will give learners a first 'strategy' for assigning stress to an unfamiliar word.

3.2
Rhythm

Having been introduced to word stress, learners will be ready to move on to the rhythm of English, which, as we have said, is characterized by the alternation of strong and weak syllables. Rhythm is a product of word stress and the way in which important items are foregrounded through their occurrence on a strong beat, and unimportant items are backgrounded by their occurrence on a weak beat.

3.2.1
Using metrical
material

8

Introductory activities

A set of activities can be built around strongly metrical material, such as rhymes, verse, limericks, and children's games. Below are a few examples:

<u>D</u> is for <u>duck</u>, with <u>spots</u> on his <u>back</u>, who <u>lives</u> in the <u>water</u>, and <u>always</u> says, <u>quack</u>.

There <u>was</u> a young <u>lady</u> of <u>Norway</u>,
Who <u>casually sat</u> in a <u>doorway</u>,
When the <u>door</u> squeezed her <u>flat</u>,
She <u>said</u> '<u>what</u> of <u>that</u>?'
That cou<u>ra</u>geous young <u>lady</u> of <u>Norway</u>.

He who fights and runs away,
Lives to fight another day.

Your selection should of course be determined by the age and interests of the learners. Adults may respond better to more sophisticated material such as famous lines from literature, or proverbs. Children will like nursery rhymes, teenagers will like the lyrics of pop songs.

Procedure

If you decide to present the material in written form, the first task should be to identify the stress patterns of the content words in the material – the nouns, verbs, adjectives and adverbs. After the stress of these has been marked, the teacher can read aloud entire lines. The learners can then fill in the other items as stressed or unstressed, using whatever notation has been introduced to them.

If you do not want to use written presentation, then tape recordings of rhymes, limericks, or short verse can be used. Their rhythm can be beaten out, conducted, or indicated by any of the notations discussed above.

The main point that you want to establish through these simple activities is the alternation in English of stronger and weaker beats, which means that English doesn't have a steady, even rhythm. It is not necessary in these early stages to involve the learners in any more detail – to mention that the stronger beats occur at equal intervals, or that function words undergo squeezing to maintain the steady beat of the stressed syllables (see 2.2.6). These points are best left to be absorbed through the listening and speaking activities learners do as they progress.

Follow-up activities

Once you've explored the rhythm of a few examples of highly metrical material, you can devise some activities in which the learners must provide words or phrases which fit into an already established pattern, a kind of rhythmic fill-in-the-blank exercise. Using material similar to that already presented, blank out a word or phrase. Give an indication of the stress pattern, and give a choice of three to four items, all of which fit the meaning of the line, but only one of which fits the required stress pattern. Here is an example:[3]

A: Dinner's ready. Come and get it.
B: What's for dinner?
A: Chicken curry.
B: What's for pudding?
A: O o O o   (apple crumble/strawberry tart/lemon pie)

A slightly more difficult task can be designed by simply leaving out the stress pattern clue; the learners have to figure out from the rhythm of the line(s) which pattern is needed and then which word(s) fit the pattern. Alternatively, you can blank out a word or·phrase (or even an entire line), provide no alternatives, and leave it to the learners to think up something appropriate that fits the meaning and the stress pattern. Here is an example using a short dialogue:

A: This is the furniture.

B: Isn't it terrible!

A: What shall we do with it?

B: _____(*possible completion*: Give it to somebody.)

The teacher doesn't need to prepare a lot of examples. This is an exercise designed to sensitize learners to word stress patterns and rhythm, not a training course for verse makers or dialogue writers, so a few examples will suffice. The last, most complicated, task may be better as a homework assignment, since individuals vary a lot in the time they need to think of suitable completions.

If you have been using verse and metrical material in the activities, it is a good idea to include more natural utterances, just to make sure that the learners don't get the idea that only English verse is rhythmical. Here are some examples of everyday sentences which happen to conform to regular metrical patterns:

It's not very easy to play the guitar.

What do you want me to do with it now?

(*Both have a strong* O o o *pattern*.)

These activities, which ask learners to find something which fits a pattern, require active involvement and include a dimension of meaning as well. They are, therefore, a departure from the usual strategy of mimicking models, choral repetition, and chanting, which can also be used. Asking learners to decide which of several possibilities fit into a pattern, asking them to classify items according to which pattern they follow, are analytical activities. They make different demands on learners from those of the mechanical activities often used. The teacher's role shifts from directing imitation exercises to that of language informant. The teacher presents the learners with a task and provides them with models of the spoken forms as they are needed; he or she also provides feedback when the task is completed. It is, of course, possible to make learners aware of the notion of stress patterns and rhythm through mechanical repetition and some learners may respond well to this approach, but if an analytical dimension can be incorporated, it will provide another level of reinforcement. Adults in particular may benefit from this. It's a matter of deciding which types of activities seem to suit the learners.

3.3

Sentence stress

In spoken English there are various ways in which a speaker gives the listener information about the relative importance of different parts of the message. One way of doing this is to put stress on the words which carry the most information. This is usually called *main sentence stress*. In this section we will discuss some ways of introducing learners to the use of stress placement in the clause or sentence. As listeners, it is essential that they are able to spot points of focus in the stream of speech; as speakers, they must highlight points in their messages, or English listeners will have difficulty in interpreting what they hear, in deciding how it relates to what has just been said and predicting what the speaker is possibly leading up to.

We have said that stress placement in utterances is linked to relative importance (see 1.5). The introduction of sentence stress will be more effective if the teacher can select a context which forces learners to grapple with this notion of 'importance'. After all, this is an abstract concept which can be quite elusive and difficult to define. Of course, one could simply say, 'When you speak, give more emphasis to the most important words', relying on concepts of 'emphasis' and 'importance' that the learners have developed already through the use of their native languages. This sounds quite straightforward, but how should they go about choosing what is most important? Every word seems important to someone who is struggling to put together a message in a new language. Indeed, the concern 'not to leave anything out' often leads to overstressing; unfluent speakers who are pausing a lot and searching for almost every word, often end up stressing every word. We need activities which make learners think about the relative importance of parts of a message.

3.3.1
Selectivity

There are two real-life situations in which restrictions on resources require a person to be selective, to include only words that are essential and to omit words that aren't. One is sending a telegram, the other is writing newspaper headlines. These situations can be used to devise activities which will involve the learners in selecting according to importance. However, since both are essentially written forms of the language, teachers will need to build in a stage incorporating speech.

Sending a telegram

Although telephone communication is quickly replacing telegrams, except in certain contexts where a written record is needed, most people are familiar with the process of sending a telegram, and most can imagine themselves having to do this at some time in their lives. In sending a telegram, one pays by the word, and the majority of people react by limiting the number of words as much as possible. Presumably the millionaires among us don't bother!

Procedure
Begin with a written message in full. This can be provided by you or written by the learners in response to a situation. Here's an example. You have gone to the airport to catch your flight home, but there is a strike and all flights are postponed for forty-eight hours. You must send a telegram to your place of work to say you will not be back on time. Now give the group a word restriction by saying either: (1) send a telegram with as few words as possible; or (2) the cost per word is x, and you have only y amount of money. When the class has prepared the telegrams, in groups, pairs, or individually, discuss which words they chose to omit and which to leave in, and why. At this point some of them may notice that they could leave out the personal pronoun, articles, prepositions, etc. Comment on this if it comes up. Mark the selected words that have been deemed important enough to pay for on the full written version. Then read it aloud, using gesture to underline the stressed words. (It is probably best not to use the same convention that has been introduced for marking word stress, to avoid confusion.) It is necessary to have this reading

aloud stage so that the teacher can point out the correlation between importance and stress when speaking. If you want to extend the activity to provide more opportunity to experiment with stress placement, proceed as follows.

Divide the class into pairs. One partner must write another full message and select the words he or she wants to 'pay' for in a telegram, marking them in some way (for instance by circling or underlining). The full message is then read aloud to the partner, who listens and writes down only the words he or she hears as stressed. The pair then check to see if results match intentions. If the partner who is transcribing needs frequent repetition, or gets it wrong too often, the teacher may intervene. Readers may also produce some strange-sounding versions, even using exaggerated stress or volume so that they end up sounding like a radio where someone is fiddling with the volume control. This unnaturalness doesn't really matter at this stage; it's more important that students should have the opportunity to make their selection and try to reflect this somehow in their spoken delivery.

Newspaper headlines

Here, the restriction which governs selection is one of space. Headlines often omit articles, auxiliary verbs, and some prepositions, in order to have more space for the 'content' words which will give the gist of the news item. There is also another convention which can be useful to the teacher; very often the very first line of the article is an expanded version of the headline.

Procedure

Collect a few examples of headlines. Be careful to avoid extreme examples of journalese, especially those headlines which consist of long sequences of words used as modifiers such as the following:

GIRL IN SHOTGUN DEATH RIDDLE

MAFIA LINK SCANDAL BREAKS[4]

Present the headlines to the class and ask them what words have been left out. Discuss why these words were considered to be non-essential by the editor. Contrast reading aloud the headline (where every word will be stressed), with reading aloud a full version, where the same words are stressed, but the others are unstressed. Learners can then devise their own headlines for news stories and events, or expand headlines and read them aloud to each other. Again, the reading aloud stage is somewhat artificial, but necessary to make the link between importance and stress. Recordings of news headlines as read aloud on radio or television can also be incorporated into the activity, providing a more realistic way to explore stress placement.

3.3.2
Shifting stress

Whether a word is 'important' or not is closely connected to its status as newly introduced, or previously introduced, in a conversation. When something is mentioned for the first time, the speaker will put stress on it, using the voice to say: 'I'm introducing this topic into our conversation.'

The second and further times the topic is mentioned or a particular word is used, it will usually not be stressed (unless the speaker feels the need to reintroduce it).[5]

An exercise for beginners

At beginners' level, it is possible to demonstrate this shift of stress using simple dialogues in which the two speakers ask each other the same question in turn. Here's an example (stressed syllables are underlined):

10

A: <u>What</u> do you <u>do</u>?
B: I'm a comp<u>u</u>ter <u>pro</u>grammer. What do <u>you</u> do?
A: I work in a sol<u>ici</u>tor's <u>off</u>ice.

When A asks the question both 'what' and 'do' will be stressed. When B asks the same question 'you' will receive the most stress. Other similar dialogues can be built around simple questions such as *How are you? What's your name? Where are you from? How many are there in your family?* (Avoid *How do you do?* as this phrase is always delivered with the same stress.) If such dialogues occur in the coursebook, then this is the ideal time to draw learners' attention to the stress placement.

Procedure

Begin by taking the role of first questioner. Indicate to a student that he or she should ask the same question of you. Listen for correct stress placement. If the student does not place stress on the appropriate word/s, indicate that something is wrong and provide a correct model. Referring to a written model, mark the stress and give a simple explanation such as: 'When A asks the question first, the most important word/s is/are _____ . But when B asks the same question y<u>ou</u> is stressed, and not the other words, because they are just repetitions.' You might also show the learners how sometimes the second occurrence can be shortened to such forms as 'And you?' or 'How about you?' as in:

A: <u>Where</u> are you <u>from</u>?
B: <u>Par</u>is. And <u>you</u>?
A: <u>Lon</u>don.

'New' words and 'old' words

The above dialogue activity is quite limited in the structures and vocabulary involved, and therefore suitable for lower levels. Here is a slightly more complicated and variable activity to explore the way stress is allocated to words according to their status as 'new' or 'old'.

Note how in the following dialogue 'sugar' is stressed by speaker A and not stressed by speaker B. B places the stress on 'brown' instead:

11

A: Could I <u>borrow</u> some <u>white sugar</u>?
B: <u>Sorry</u>, I <u>only</u> have <u>brown</u> sugar.

An activity can also be devised to draw the learners' attention to the way the stress shifts in a noun phrase from noun and adjective to just the new/different adjective.

Procedure

First, prepare lists of ingredients for some simple recipes. Then prepare lists of 'items in stock' or 'items in the store-cupboard'. In both lists use some foods which exist in different forms. For example, chocolate can be 'plain' or 'milk'; flour, bread or sugar can be 'white' or 'brown', and so on. These lists can be used in several ways.

1 To build short dialogues between friends/neighbours/flatmates, etc.

2 To build short dialogues between customer and shopkeeper, as in:

A: Do you <u>have</u> any <u>double</u> <u>cream</u>?
B: <u>No</u>, we're <u>out</u> of <u>stock</u>. But we <u>do</u> have <u>single</u> cream.
A: <u>No</u>, I <u>must</u> have <u>double</u> cream.

3 To play a matching game. The class is divided into two groups. One group has the list of ingredients for specific recipes; the other has the list of available items. The 'cooks' must circulate, asking the others questions until they find someone who has the ingredients they need.

4 To do a pair activity. One student has the recipe (or two or three different ones); the other has the list of items in the store-cupboard. Together they must decide what they can cook, or what menu they can have for a dinner party.

For all the above activities, the restriction that the students may not simply look at each others' lists will promote exchange of information.

Whichever of these possibilities is selected, the teacher can present a model first, and then, while the activity is proceeding, monitor the placement of stress, calling a halt and correcting if necessary. As the activity winds down, the learners should be encouraged to listen to their colleagues and monitor their stress placement. Alternatively, the teacher can set up the activity and then call a halt to explain the operation of stress, if the students don't use it appropriately.

3.4
Weak forms

Weak forms should be introduced after the basic points about word stress, rhythm, and sentence stress have been covered. There are many weak forms which are used in English (at the end of Chapter 4 there is a list of the most frequent). It is probably wise to choose one or two common weak forms and construct an awareness-building exercise around them, rather than overload learners with a long list. One also needs an activity or example which will clearly demonstrate the reasons behind the use of weak forms.

'The house that Jack built'

The English chanting game 'The house that Jack built' has definite potential as a focus for the introduction of the notion of weak forms. The relative clause marker 'that' is always pronounced weakly in the chant. Indeed it is always pronounced weakly in English, so it is an especially good example of a weak form. (Note: 'that' as a demonstrative pronoun, as in 'that is my book', never has a weak pronunciation.) The chant has some other advantages: the vocabulary is basic, simple, and concrete; it is therefore easy to build up the chant using picture cues. Most importantly, the word 'that' is clearly 'unimportant'; the important words are the new names, objects, and actions: chased, cat, killed, ate, etc.

Procedure

Begin by introducing this chant by saying, for example, that every English-speaking person learns it as a child. If you are teaching adults or young adults who may react negatively to learning a children's chant, then you can introduce it by pointing out that there is no limit to how many words an English sentence can have, and say that you are going to demonstrate this to them using a children's game. Using picture or word cues, build up two or three verses. A tape recording can be useful. Make sure the learners are using the appropriate rhythm and stress patterns.

This is the house that Jack built.
This is the malt* that lay in the house that Jack built.
This is the rat,
That ate the malt
That lay in the house that Jack built.
This is the cat,
That killed the rat,
That ate the malt
That lay in the house that Jack built.
This is the dog
That worried the cat,
That killed the rat,
That ate the malt
That lay in the house that Jack built.

After you've built up a few stanzas, draw the learners' attention to the word 'that', asking them first to give its pronunciation alone (with the full value of the vowel). Now draw their attention to the pronunciation of 'that' in the chant. Ask if they hear any difference. The difference is of course in the vowel. (If you have not already mentioned the 'schwa' vowel, then you can do so now.) Now ask about the role of 'that' in the chant. Possible prompts are: 'Is it an important word? Is it repeated? Does it have a meaning like rat, house, cat, killed?'

At this point you could put two lists of words on the board, 'meaning words' and 'grammar or function words'. If you have used a visual representation of the rhythm, then draw learners' attention to the fact that 'that' is always unstressed.

It is at this stage that you may want to introduce the term *weak form* to them. It is also useful to have an opposite as well. *Strong form* often occurs in the literature. *Citation form* is also used, referring to the form a word has when it is 'cited' in isolation. *Full form* is useful as an opposite, especially since you can use it to talk about full vowels as well as full forms. ('Strong vowels' or 'citation form vowels' don't work as well.) A

* *Note*: malt is a grain (usually barley) which is used in making beer. Since this is a rare word, you might want to substitute 'corn' or 'rice' or 'grain'.

gesture that can be used to indicate or remind learners about weak forms can be introduced at this stage. Forefinger and thumb brought increasingly close together in a kind of measuring gesture conveys the idea that these words are reduced or made smaller in some way. To round off the activity, you could do any of the following:

1 Provide a few simple sentences with 'that' relative clauses and ask learners to repeat or read aloud, making sure they use schwa in the word 'that'.

2 Ask them to make up sentences about their personal possessions, such as: 'This is the pullover that I bought yesterday.' Sentences like these, where 'that' stands in for the object in the second clause, are particularly useful, because 'that' can be optionally omitted ('This is the pullover I bought yesterday'). If you point this out, it will underline the 'unimportance' of this word.

In order to avoid learners pronouncing 'that' with schwa when it is functioning as a demonstrative, it may be advisable to draw their attention to the two uses – 'that' as demonstrative and 'that' as relative clause marker. The chant itself provides a simple way to do this because the first word can easily be changed to 'that': 'That is the house that Jack built.' We now have the two 'thats' together. Without using any terminology, you can point out that the first is a 'pointing word' and is always pronounced with the full vowel as in 'cat', and that the second always links parts of a sentence and is always pronounced with schwa.

Weak 'and'

Another word which can be used as a first example of a weak form is the conjunction 'and'. Here are three ways to work on the pronunciation of 'and'.

1 At a selected point in the lesson, ask the learners to pronounce the word in isolation. Then give them a short phrase or sentence with 'and' to pronounce. If you get a full pronunciation with the vowel /a/ as in 'cat' and the final consonant, stop them and repeat the phrase or sentence yourself, using the weak form. Ask them if they hear the difference. When they do, introduce the term *weak form* and/or the gesture mentioned above. Give a brief explanation such as: 'This is a very small word and English people usually say it very quickly.' (Be careful that none of your phrases or sentences have a word beginning with 'd' after 'and', because it is more difficult to illustrate the omission of final 'd' in 'and'.)

2 Exploit written forms such as:
fish 'n chips
bacon 'n eggs
salt 'n pepper
Ask the learners why they think 'n' is used. Prompt if necessary by contrasting the pronunciations with weak 'and', and full 'and'. Give terms, the gesture, and a brief explanation as above. This strategy may work well for learners in an English environment who may have actually seen these written forms.

3 Ask the learners to start a chain sentence in which nouns or verbs are connected with 'and' in a sentence of potentially infinite length. The objects in the classroom or favourite foods are a simple choice. One student starts: 'I can see a desk.' The next student repeats and adds another item: 'I can see a desk and a lamp'. At an appropriate point, and before the memory load becomes too great, draw their attention to their pronunciation of 'and'. When they are repeating what the previous students have said, they should really be using the weak form. As they make their own addition a full pronunciation is acceptable.

After any of the above activities, you can refer the students to their coursebooks and challenge them to find an occurrence of the word 'and' that merits a full pronunciation. They probably won't find any; if they do it will probably be underlined, or in large capitals.

Weak 'of'

'Of' is another word which is often weakened. The spellings 'cuppa' and 'pinta' which are often used in advertisements can be used like the 'n' spelling to draw learners' attention to the schwa vowel and the deletion of 'f'. Follow the procedure outlined above in 2. If you do find examples of these spellings, be sure to mention that they are restricted to certain kinds of writing. As a follow-up, the learners can be asked to search out phrases with 'of' in their text books, make a list, and practise the pronunciation with weak 'of' in pairs. Alternatively, pronunciation practice can be introduced into any vocabulary work which involves phrases with 'of'. (Classifiers are a good example: bunch of grapes, pair of shoes, group of people, etc.) Learners should get used to hearing such phrases with a weak 'of'. As a *production* target, it is not necessary to insist on the deletion of 'f', but the weakening of the vowel to schwa should be insisted on.

Having gone through one or more of these exercises with the students, you will have made them aware of the phenomenon of weak forms through one or two of the most common examples. You will also have introduced a term and/or gesture to use, to remind them of this aspect of English. You can then add to the list of weak forms as they occur in the teaching materials you are using.

**3.5
Intonation**

Upon hearing an unknown language, most people seem to react not so much to different sounds (these may not even be noticed) as to the intonation and rhythm of the language. It's very common for people to say something like, 'Language X is very melodic/sing-song', and equally common for people to claim that their own language is 'very flat, and doesn't have much melody'. This reaction is perhaps an indication of the largely unconscious level at which intonation (and rhythm) operate, since *all* languages have intonation and a characteristic rhythmic pattern.

It would seem sensible to exploit in the classroom this tendency to compare the new and native languages as a means of building awareness of intonation in English. In teaching situations where the class members share the same native language, or where only two or three languages dominate, some comparative activities can be carried out. Here are two possibilities.

3.5.1
Comparative
activities

Dialogues

(a) Select a tape recording of a short exchange such as the following (two friends are talking about a mutual acquaintance):

A: Is Mary French?
B: No, she's from Switzerland.
A: Which part?
B: Geneva, I think.

Ask the learners to translate the dialogue into their native languages. (It's wise to have a few back-up dialogues prepared in case there are any translation difficulties.) Have the learners rehearse and tape-record their dialogues. Now play the English and other-language recordings in turn and begin to question the learners about similarities and differences in how the speakers use their voices. Questions may be open-ended: 'Do the voices have the same melody?' or more specific: 'Does the English voice go up or down in the first question?' or 'Does the speaker who answers the first question in the (language X) dialogue begin with his/her voice very high, or keep his/her voice high?' In the discussion avoid technical terms such as 'pitch', or 'intonation', unless the learners have encountered these before or offer them themselves. The terms 'melody', 'rise/fall', 'up/down', 'high/low', are appropriate for discussing intonation. Similarly, the terms 'beat/rhythm' will be useful if these have already been introduced for work on rhythm, especially when aided by tapping or conducting hand gestures. Don't attempt to describe in any detail differences that are noticed – use the activity to sensitize learners to these features. Make sure that your own stance is seen by the learners to be an exploratory one by expressing interest in whatever remarks they make.

(b) A follow-up activity can be developed around the dialogues by asking some of the learners if they can hum the dialogue instead of actually saying the words. Start by doing this yourself and then ask for volunteers. If the humming attempts are successful, have the students record two or three hummed dialogues. Have a few hummed English dialogues prepared. Play all the dialogues to the class without identifying which language they are supposed to be. Can the class tell which is which? If they manage to do this, ask what helped them. Several features may be mentioned:

number of syllables
overall high/low pitch
length of utterances
rhythm – alternation of stressed and unstressed syllables
I recognized _____ 's voice!

Accept all of these suggestions, but show particular enthusiasm for suggestions which seem to demonstrate that pitch (and also rhythmic) features have been noticed.

If the dialogues cannot be identified, then the conclusion is quite a comforting one – the voice is used in the same way in English and the other language(s) in these particular situations.

It is possible that trying to hum words may make learners feel self-conscious. Also, it may be that the translation, preparation and recording of dialogues in class is too time-consuming. These complications can be avoided by pre-recording the native language as well as the English language dialogues.

**3.5.2
Using 'fillers'**

Another way to develop awareness of the role of intonation is to exploit the use of various sounds used in spoken language which are not words, but convey meaning through non-lexical means, principally through intonation pattern. Such sounds (sometimes called *non-lexical fillers*) are often used in English and other languages to express approval/disapproval, interest, assent/dissent, and to say, 'I've heard what you said and I'm thinking about it.' When written, they are often represented as 'uh huh', 'um', 'er', 'oh', 'ah'. 'Well' is often used in the same ways.

Wordless information

Procedure
To introduce the activity to the class, select pairs of learners and set them a situation to act out. For example:

 15

(a) A and B are flatmates. A wants to redecorate the flat, and puts various ideas to B, who reacts with enthusiasm to some suggestions, but not all.
(b) A and B are friends. A has just returned from her holiday and is showing B her holiday photos, and telling her about her experiences.

Ask the pairs of learners to act out their situations for the class, or you may want to do this as pairwork. Now introduce the restriction that B must react without using any words. B may only use sounds. Give the possible English 'noises' to the students if they aren't aware of them already ('mm', 'ah', 'ooo'). The activity can be organized as pairwork or each pair may be asked to perform for the class.

A discussion should follow in which the class is asked to comment on:

— what sounds were used to replace full sentences or utterances in the first set of role plays
— what feelings were shown by B's monosyllabic responses
— what facial expression and gestures were used to accompany or reinforce the non-lexical 'noises'.

Keep the discussion fairly informal. Learners should be intrigued by just how much information can be conveyed without words. This activity can also be given a comparative dimension by asking students to perform similar situations in their own languages. This stage will probably reveal some common uses of particular intonation patterns across languages (for example, a high rising tone to show extreme interest in what the other person has said).

**3.5.3
Using games**

Language games can also provide the opportunity to make learners aware of intonation. Here are two possibilities:

Getting warmer!

This is a 'finding' game often played by young children. In the language classroom the game is organized in the following way. An object is hidden in the classroom. One member of the class is chosen to try to find it – this could be the teacher in the first instance. The nominated finder is of course not present when the object is hidden. Everyone else knows where it is, and may help the finder, but only by giving clues about how close the finder is to the hidden object by saying 'warmer' if the finder moves nearer the object in the search, or 'colder' if the finder moves further away from it. However, there are really more than two ways of helping because the amount of excitement and anticipation in the voices (as shown by high pitch, volume, and sharp rises and falls) as opposed to disappointment (shown by sudden drops in pitch level and volume and general lowering of the pitch of the voice) can give the finder a great deal of information about how close he or she is getting to the object. As the game proceeds, the learners will probably naturally use these patterns, but if they don't seem to be exploiting them to the full, then the teacher can get involved. At an appropriate point, say after a particularly efficient finding, the teacher can make a comment like: 'You're using your voice a lot to help, aren't you?' It's unnecessary to specify exactly how this is being done, but if the students seem intrigued then the teacher can make some further comments referring to the features mentioned above.

Wild guess!

This is a simple guessing game in which students must give short answers to general information questions. The teacher needs to prepare a set of everyday knowledge questions, appropriate to the level and interests of the class members, in a multiple choice or open answer format. A questioner is selected and students are assigned answering turns. Start with a dry run by asking several students to answer some sample questions. Introduce the convention that the person whose turn it is *must* answer – they cannot pass their turn. Start the game with the class divided into teams, or by giving each individual a turn. Award ten points for each correct answer and deduct ten points for each incorrect answer. At an appropriate point, introduce the notion of a 'wild guess' versus an 'educated guess'. The best way to do this is to wait until a student gives an answer in a way which shows he or she is fairly certain of its correctness (usually shown by low falling intonation and/or a facial expression of certainty), or when a student is obviously making a wild guess (usually shown by high rising intonation, a doubtful facial expression, etc.). Make a comment such as: 'That sounds like a wild guess to me. You're not very sure at all, are you?' or: 'You sound like you really know you're correct', to introduce the notion of degrees of certainty/uncertainty.

Let the game proceed and continue to draw learners' attention to this use of intonation by making comments at appropriate points, such as: 'You're really making a wild guess, aren't you?'; 'Is that a wild guess?'; 'You sound quite sure about that.' The team or individual with the most points at the end of the game wins. The teacher can also keep a record of how many wild guesses and educated guesses were made by individuals or teams. The aim of this aspect of the game is to make learners aware of how much information they can convey or 'give away' through intonation.

3.5.4
Using drama

Drama techniques also have great potential for initial explorations of intonation. Consider the following dialogue:

A: What are you doing here?
B: Waiting for somebody.
A: Have you been waiting long?
B: About half an hour.
A: Why don't you sit down?
B: I'm OK. I don't mind standing.

There are several possible contexts. A could be a security guard who is suspicious of B's behaviour, or an acquaintance who has accidentally run into B and is either quite surprised and glad to see B, or may actually regret the chance encounter and is making conversation in a rather uncomfortable manner. The setting could be, for instance, a hotel lobby, a station, or a public park. The ambiguity of the dialogue can be exploited in order to explore intonation.[6]

Matching interpretations

The following variation on this activity is suitable for students who are at a level of competence in English where they can describe people, feelings and situations.

Procedure
Divide the learners into small groups and give each a written copy of the same dialogue. Assign each group a different set of roles, participants, setting, and participant attitudes, as in the example above. Students prepare the dialogues and perform them for the rest of the class. The class is told what the different 'assignments' were and must try to match each performance with the given assignments. Alternatively, the teacher may present recordings or videos of the dialogues acted out in the different ways by English speakers. Guide the discussion by focusing on features such as intonation, volume, speed of delivery, and facial expression, linking these to aspects of the setting, situation, and identity of the participants. Avoid providing the learners with complex attitude labels like 'irritated', 'reassuring', 'considerate', unless they explicitly ask for them. It is also important to keep the discussion as concrete as possible, for example: 'A doesn't really care about B at all, and wishes she hadn't met him and will try to get away and stop talking as quickly as possible.' If there is disagreement about which performance had which assignments, encourage the students to act out the dialogues again to demonstrate what they mean.

One advantage of using drama activities like these is that there is a clear demonstration of the way intonation interacts with gestural and lexical features, which is often lost when only audio-taped material is used. Everyone can spot the phoniness of the exaggerated friendly tone of voice adopted by, say, a sales assistant when the facial expression does not convey the same degree of friendliness. If this interaction of pitch and gesture exists in the normal use of spoken language, then why should these features be disassociated in the classroom? Why restrict ourselves to taped material whenever intonation is the focus of the lesson? A more sensible approach would be to combine the type of material used: tapes (to help learners to concentrate on the rise and fall of the pitch), video, and the whole range of acting techniques (drama, role play and simulations). In real encounters with English speakers learners will call upon all possible means and strategies to communicate (gesture, mime, facial expression, intonation, etc.). There is no reason why classroom activities should attempt to tease apart the threads of what is a highly complex fabric, or give prominence to one feature to the exclusion of the others, as has often been the case in some teaching materials for intonation.

3.5.5
General remarks

It must be stressed that the exercises and activities described in this section are not designed to teach particular intonation patterns. They exploit to a large extent what is common to the use of intonation in most languages. The aims of these introductory activities are: first, to make students aware that they can often rely on the ways they use intonation in their own languages when speaking English, but that they should watch out for differences; second, to persuade them that the area of intonation is something that deserves their attention because they can do so much with it when speaking English. Any opportunity that arises in the classroom can be used to the same ends, whether it is a spontaneous answer a student has given to a question, or the use of a pattern that has been focused on through one of the above activities in audio or video recordings that are being used in class.

In carrying out the activities, the teacher should avoid an approach based on rules, or one that attempts to link a particular intonation pattern with a particular meaning or attitude. Some general guidelines and tendencies can be provided for English intonation, but the rules which govern its use are so varied, so dependent on context, or so abstract in nature, that their presentation in great detail would soon confuse or overwhelm learners. Try to simplify matters. Rather than providing a complex set of attitude labels such as 'bored', 'slightly interested', 'enthusiastic', 'angry', 'irritated', 'furious', provide a cover term instead ('interest' or 'anger' for the above examples). Then operate with points on a scale, or a system of pluses or minuses. For example, in using the drama technique outlined above, elicit scores from the students, and use the mechanisms of consensus opinion and totalling of points awarded to show contrasts in the acted-out versions. It is important that learners realize that intonation is a 'more or less' situation, a matter of degree, and sometimes very individual and situation-specific. There is *not* a set of *exact* complex alternatives which must be exactly imitated to achieve a desired effect. An initial approach which is open and flexible in this way and builds upon what the learners bring to the task from their own languages will prepare them, at later stages in their development of communication skills in English, to work on specific uses of intonation in English which *do* seem to be crucial for effective and efficient communication in particular situations. We will look at some of these in Chapter 4.

3.6
The sounds

3.6.1
Perception of sounds

All learners expect English to have new and different sounds – in fact, they may even already know about a few of the most distinctive sounds, like the 'th' sounds in '*the*' and '*th*ree', which are actually very rare in the languages of the world. So, in a sense, learners come to their task with a basic awareness in this area; they are aware of the fact that they will have to produce new sounds, although they will probably be completely unaware of aspects such as intonation and rhythm.

However, in the area of sounds the word 'awareness' has a very special meaning. Many of the learners' problems will be *perceptual* – they will be completely unaware that a sound they hear, or are making, is not the same as the sound English people use. People tend to hear the sounds of a new language in terms of the sounds of their mother tongue. Let's look briefly at the nature of such perception problems.

As we are learning to speak our first language, we learn what the significant sounds are and how to deal with any variations of them that we come across. In other words, we learn what to pay attention to and what to ignore. Young babies, before they even say their first word, experiment with making a variety of sounds in which the air flows through the nose ('nasal' sounds like *m*, and *n*). But after a period of experimentation, children in an English-speaking environment seem to notice that there are only three 'important' nasal sounds in English (*m*, *n*, and si*ng*); these are the only sounds of this type they need to listen for. This leads to a three-way classification system being set up in the sound centres of the brain and, once this has been established, all nasal sounds which are heard are examined and sorted according to the three categories. The sorting system is a very powerful mechanism, and has been likened to a 'sieve'.

Each language has its own distinctive set of categories, and part of the process of learning a new language is learning what the significant sounds are. This may involve setting up a system with, say, four nasal sounds and getting used to recognizing the new sound instead of ignoring it, treating it as a trivial variant, or 'counting' it as a member or example of one of the mother tongue's three-term system. The nature of the task is basically similar to that of the fruit sorter who has been used to sorting apples into three sizes, A, B, and C, and suddenly has to begin to sort the same crop of apples into four sizes. Consequently, in sorting two apples which would both formerly have fitted into category C, one of them must now be put in category C and the other in the new category D. The process of adjustment can be a difficult one.

The traditional way of helping someone to perceive sounds according to a new set of categories is to give them plenty of opportunities to hear all the members of the new system. The new sounds should be heard together with the 'familiar' sounds from the mother tongue; two new sounds should be heard together so that the difference between them will be learnt. It can also be helpful to hear a new sound together with a familiar sound. The sounds should be heard in different combinations, in different sequences and positions (for example, after a particular vowel or preceding it, at the end of words, and at the beginning of words) and *not* only in isolation, because this isn't the way we hear sounds. Learners should also be given the opportunity to hear sounds substituted for each other in the same surroundings, i.e. in *minimal pairs*. A minimal pair is a pair of words which differ only in the two sounds being focused on. 'Met' and 'net' are a minimal pair which contrasts /m/ and /n/; 'road' and 'load' are a minimal pair which contrasts /r/ and /l/.

3.6.2
Minimal pair practice

First, select the sounds you need to work on. This can be done by referring to the information in Part Two, or by giving a diagnostic test to check on learners' perception of sounds.

Many of the pairs of consonants that will cause problems are pairs that differ in only one aspect – that of *voicing*. Voicing refers to the vibration of the vocal cords as a sound is made. This vibration gives the sound a buzzing quality. There are many pairs of English consonants that differ only in this feature:

/p/ and /b/ (*P*ete, *b*eat)   /θ/ and /ð/ (*th*ink, *th*e)
/f/ and /v/ (*f*ast, *v*ast)   /tʃ/ and /dʒ/ (*ch*oke, *j*oke)
/ʃ/ and /ʒ/ (*sh*un, vi*s*ion)   /k/ and /g/ (*c*ore, *g*ore)
/t/ and /d/ (*t*o, *d*o)   /s/ and /z/ (*S*ue, *z*oo)

In each case the second sound has voicing, the first does not. (Demonstrate this to yourself by making each pair; you should hear the buzzing quality of the second. You may also be able to *feel* the difference by placing your hand on the front of your throat – for the voiced sounds you can feel the slight vibration.)

Several of the pairs of vowels that will cause perception problems differ only in that one is a *monothong* and the other a *diphthong*. These are the two types of vowels in English. In making monothongs the tongue and lips assume a particular position and hold it; in making diphthongs, there is a gradual change in lip and tongue position during the sound. (Demonstrate this to yourself by saying the vowels in 'can' and 'coin' – the first is a monothong, the second is a diphthong.) There are five English diphthongs:

/ai/ (s*igh*)   /au/ (n*ow*)   /ɔi/ (b*oy*)   /ei/ (s*ay*)   /ou/ (s*o*)

Learners may not be able to distinguish two of these diphthongs (for example /ou/ from /au/); a diphthong from a monothong (for example /ɔ/ in l*aw* from /ou/ in l*ow*); or they may not be able to hear the difference between two monothongs (for example /ɪ/ in *it* from /ɛ/ in b*et*).

Basic format

When you have selected the sounds that need to be worked on, prepare sets of minimal pairs.[7] Worksheets can be prepared for the students with the pairs of words beside each other. As the teacher pronounces one of the pair, the learners circle or tick the word they think they heard. It is important to provide immediate feedback, and to give those who chose the wrong word a chance to hear both words again. The teacher may choose to slightly exaggerate the production of the sounds to help the learners, by lengthening the sound or using very explicit careful articulation, but it is vital that this be followed by a more natural production of the words. It is also important to vary the position and surroundings of the target sound. For example, /t/ can occur initially, finally, and medially in English words and also with other consonants in clusters, as in 'tip', 'pit', 'trip', 'crept', etc. It is important that students learn to recognize a sound in all the positions in which it occurs in English because there are positional variants of a particular sound. For example, English /t/ at the beginning of words or at the beginning of a stressed syllable is characterized by a strong puff of air before the vowel is produced (this is known as *aspiration*). This is not true of /t/ in combination with /s/ as in 'stick' (see 4.3.3) and the puff of air is 'optional' at the end of words.

Minimal pair practice can be done with a tape recording of the word pairs, but again immediate feedback should be given and the tape replayed to give another opportunity for the learners to hear the sounds. The advantage of using a tape is that the model will be unchanging – the tape cannot exaggerate or distort successive models as the teacher can.

3.6.3
Variations on the basic format

Listening for a specified word

Another possibility is to give one word on the worksheet and to ask the learners to identify it from a set of spoken possibilities. For example, the word 'pit' is on the worksheet; the teacher (or tape) presents and gives a label for three options: one–'pet'; two–'pit'; three–'Pete'. The students must select the correct word from the three stimuli and write its number beside it (in this case 2) which means: 'The second word I heard was "pit".'

Which order?

The learners' worksheet has sets of words in twos or threes. The teacher produces each set and the learners must indicate in what order they have just heard the words by writing the appropriate number next to the words. For example, if the teacher reads out 'pet, pit, Pete' in that order, the learners must indicate the order on their worksheet:

2   3   1
pit Pete pet

Write the word you hear

It is possible to ask learners to write what they hear, as in a dictation exercise, or words can be given with one or two letters missing in each, so that learners have to listen and fill in the missing letter(s). This should not be seen as a spelling exercise and the teacher must be prepared to accept any sequence of letters which correctly corresponds to the sequence of sounds heard. For example, both 'meet' and 'meat' must be accepted for that sequence of consonant-vowel-consonant, but not 'mite' or 'meit'. This last example reveals a pitfall in this type of exercise. 'Ei' *is* a possible spelling for the vowel in the sequence (for example, 'receive') but m-e-i-t does not happen to be an English word. The teacher can react by saying, 'Yes, that is a possible sequence', but will probably want to point out that only 'meet' and 'meat' are real English words. The exercise could easily lose its focus on perception and become more like a lesson on the English spelling system.

This pitfall has its source in the complexities of English spelling and for this reason it is probably best to limit the sounds that are focused on to consonants (vowel spellings are too variable) and to those that are more or less invariably represented by a single letter or letter sequence in English. This restriction limits the consonants to 'd, f, j, m, n, p, v, y, z'. ('b, k, l' also stand for only one sound, with a few rare exceptions.)

Despite these complicating factors, this 'write what you hear' type of exercise is valuable for training learners to hear the order in which consonant sounds occur in clusters, a task which can be difficult in certain cases. For example, the learners have ea __ before them; the teacher produces either 'east' or 'eats' and the learners must fill in the letters in the right order, or, alternatively, write the entire word, with no cue provided.

Perception work can also be done in a purely oral mode. Indeed, it is necessary to use an oral presentation for some types of exercises in order to avoid both the clues and the spelling interference that can result if the learners see written forms.

Which sound?

Minimal pairs are devised for a particular target sound(s). The sounds are labelled 'a' and 'b' or 'one' and 'two'. The teacher models the sounds, identifying them with a label: sound one – 'bat'; sound two – 'pat'. Then he or she produces one of the pair and asks which sound was heard. To do this task the learners must hold an 'image' of the two sounds in their memory, and then decide which of the two they have heard.

Same or different?

The learners hear two words in succession and have to say whether they heard the same word twice, or two different words said one after the other. This type of perception exercise is particularly well-suited to situations where learners cannot distinguish two English sounds because in their native language these two sounds are simply variants of one another. For example, a Japanese speaker, upon hearing 'road' and 'load', may well say 'same' because in Japanese these two sounds actually 'count' as the same sound. In English they are two different sounds.

Odd one out?

The teacher says a series of three or four words and asks the students to identify which, if any, was the odd one out. Again each word needs an identifying number. The teacher may say 'bit, bit, pit, bit'; learners should respond with 'three' because that was the odd one out.

How many times did you hear it?

In this task, learners are given a sound they must listen for. The teacher then says a short phrase in which the sound occurs at least once. They must listen carefully and count the number of occurrences they hear. For example, the target sound may be the vowel as in b*i*t and the phrase 'I read it in *The Times*' (in which it occurs twice). As the learners get used to the exercise, and begin to feel confident in their abilities, the teacher may surprise them by saying a phrase which doesn't have any occurrences of the target sound.

**3.6.4
Amount of
perception work**

In asking learners to do perception exercises we should keep in mind the assumptions behind these tasks. The basic assumption is, as we have said, that without such training they would be lost in a sea of sound, unaware of what they are aiming at. What we are trying to do through perceptual training is 're-tune' the ears, so that learners will be able to tune into sounds not available to them before (rather like tuning into a new broadcasting wavelength with a more powerful receiver in the radio).

One important question is *how much* perceptual training is needed to bring about this re-tuning? The answer is that it depends on the learner and the learning environment. We will discuss some of the factors involved below.

Let us consider the *learner* first. As we saw in Chapter 1, some individuals are better at perceiving new sounds than others. It is simply a matter of inbuilt ability or aptitude. Also, there is some evidence which suggests that our ability to perceive new sounds can disappear or deteriorate through lack of use. In other words, if one isn't exposed to a new language for a long while the perceptive abilities begin to atrophy. Learners who have constant and repeated experience of hearing new languages may maintain their discriminatory powers, and the more recent the exposure, the more likely that the perceptive abilities will be 'fit'. Those who have had little experience which is not very recent may 'lose' their abilities.

Another factor is the *amount of exposure* to the language. It may be that the only thing which will lead to a 'permanent' re-tuning is long-term experience and exposure to the new language's sounds. In one experiment[8] it was found that it is fairly easy to bring about modifications in perception through training exercises, but it was not clear whether these modifications were in any way permanent. So, in planning and carrying out perception training, we must bear this in mind and expect learners to show some regression.

A third factor is that of *attitude and motivation*. Learning to perceive a new sound may in some cases be 'an act of will'. You listen to a bit of the new language and try to hear differences between sounds, but two sounds which your teacher *tells* you are different sound exactly the same to you. You must believe they are different, and more importantly, that sometime in the future you *will* be able to hear the two as separate sounds. If you don't have faith or decide not to bother, then you probably won't make the effort necessary to re-tune.

**3.6.5
Planning and
organization**

If the teacher takes the points above into account, then some simple guidelines for perception work emerge. First of all, learners who are surrounded by the new language will probably not need as much perception work as those who have only classroom exposure to the language. Young children may not need much programmed help in this area, but may be able to progress well if the differences are pointed out to them and they are reminded about crucial sound contrasts as they occur in materials and language models. Adults, on the other hand, must be prepared for a large amount of effort in this area, and should realize that it may take them a long time before they can easily recognize the essential sounds and contrasts.

Because perception work requires a lot of concentration in an area which is usually very unconsciously controlled by speakers, work should be done in short spurts. 'Little and often' is an appropriate rule of thumb, and learners who are working on their own should be told to take frequent breaks and not to work on sound contrasts for too long a stretch.

Another question is what type of materials, models, and form of classroom configurations should be used. Should perception training be done in the classroom with the teacher as producer, or with tape-recorded models, or in the language laboratory? Because we are asking people to pay attention to sound, it might seem sensible to remove interference from the other senses – this would aid concentration. So, work from tapes in the classroom or the language laboratory would be ideal. But it may be that vision plays a role in auditory perception – seeing the shape of the lips or the amount of tension in the facial muscles may help in distinguishing one sound from another. 'I can't hear without my glasses' is a frequently heard comment from people who wear glasses. Research has shown that looking at the speaker contributes to listening comprehension.[9] Since this is a possibility, it might be unwise to deprive learners of cues they need and will normally have (except in the case of speaking on the phone). Perhaps the best course of action is to mix the type of perception training, sometimes using tape models, sometimes using teacher-produced models.

If the teacher decides that a fair amount of perception training needs to be done, it becomes particularly important to vary the type of training, to make it as interesting as possible and to use a variety of models. One way of varying perception work is to develop game activities or introduce a competitive dimension. One possibility is 'Phonetic Bingo'.[10]

Phonetic Bingo

As in any bingo game, the players each have a board divided into squares, each occupied by a simple picture representing a word. The 'caller' has a set of cards which have the same pictures as are on the board plus some distractors – cards with word-pictures which do not occur on any of the boards. The caller shuffles the cards, and calls them out one by one. If a player has a square that matches on his or her board, he or she claims the card and covers that square with it. The first player to reach a specified goal (the entire board covered, a complete horizontal, vertical or diagonal row, all corner squares covered) is the winner. In phonetic bingo words are selected to test the perception of the sounds in English. For example, a card with a picture of a mouse and one with a picture of a mouth can be included. If the caller calls out 'mouse' and a learner claims it, believing it to be on his board by mistaking 'mouse' for 'mouth', then this reveals a difficulty in distinguishing /s/ as in mass in word final position from /θ/ as in moth in word final position. A new dimension of skill in accurate perception of sounds has been incorporated into a game which is usually won through good luck alone.

As with any type of perception practice, immediate feedback is important. The game allows for this very naturally. When a player claims a card and the caller hands it to him or her, any mismatch or mistake will be immediately obvious. If two or more players claim simultaneously, then the settling of the dispute will reveal their problems to the learners.

If the game includes all of the important sound contrasts of English, then it is a very useful and efficient way of diagnosing sound problems. Alternatively, the teacher can construct special games around problem areas already identified. For example, a game can be devised for vowel sounds only or for problematic consonants and consonant clusters.

**3.6.6
The 'most
important sound
in English'**

There is one English sound that all learners must be made aware of at a very early stage – the neutral vowel used in unstressed syllables and weak forms – the 'schwa' vowel. It should be among the first sounds that you draw to learners' attention, whether through imitation, correction, or perception work. You also need a symbol or sign for schwa, and even if you don't use any other phonetic symbols, there are two good reasons for introducing the symbol for schwa (ə). First, there is no letter that only represents schwa in the alphabet, and second, *every* vowel letter in English can represent schwa. The following examples illustrate this:

*a*bout   pock*e*t   pup*i*l   c*o*ntain   circ*u*s

Introducing schwa

Use some striking way to introduce this sound to your learners. For example, you can ask any of the following questions:

What is the most frequent sound in English?
What is the most important sound?
What sound occurs in almost every English word with more than two syllables?

Demonstrate the sound and ask the learners to reproduce it. When you think that they can hear it and discriminate it from other vowels, do some exercises that will persuade them of the frequency of schwa. You can do one of the following:

1 Say or play a short text, and ask them to listen for and count the occurrences of schwa.

2 Select a written text at random, or ask them to select one from their coursebook. Read it aloud and count the occurrences of schwa. Invariably they will not find them all, and your point about the frequency of schwa will have been made, as well as the point that any vowel letter can represent this sound.

In order for learners to speak English with correct stress and rhythm and to pronounce words so that they can be identified by English listeners, schwa is essential. Even if you do work on no other sound, some attention will probably need to be devoted to schwa.

**3.7
Linkage and
speech
simplifications**

One way to make learners aware of the phenomenon of linkage is to exploit a convention common to written English and many other languages – that words are written as units, separated from other words by a space.

51

This has not always been the case in written language; ancient Greek and Latin inscriptions on stone, runic inscriptions on wood, and old Anglo-Saxon inscriptions were all written without spaces between words or sentences. But more recently all literate members of most societies (certainly those using alphabetic scripts) have used the convention of putting a space between words. Influenced by this convention of written language, most people assume that there is an equivalent to this boundary in the spoken language, that a period of silence separates spoken words. As explained in 2.2.4, this is not the case. Rather than boundaries of silence, there are sound mergers (where the final sound of one word can affect the initial sound of another word) and sound insertions (where a sound which belongs to neither word acts as a link between them, creating a kind of transition between a word and its neighbour).

Identical neighbouring sounds

Let's look first at a way of exploring with learners what happens when the same sound occurs both at the end of one word and at the beginning of the next word.

Procedure
Begin by writing on the board a few short phrases in which two identical sounds abut:

I want to.

He had done it.

I feel like . . .

(It's slightly easier to see that there are two identical neighbouring sounds in a written presentation.) Now ask the class to count the number of sounds in each word, and write the numbers above the word, so that you will have on the board:

1　4　2
I want to

Now play a tape recording of the phrase or pronounce it yourself, being careful to merge the final 't' of *want* with the initial 't' of *to*. In other words, do not release the tongue contact for the first 't' but hold it for the 't' in *to*. Ask the group to count how many sounds there are in the phrase. The question should now arise: 'Are there two 't's' or only one?' It certainly sounds as if there is only one. (The exact phonetic evidence shows that there is an extra long 't'.) Ask the learners if they can pronounce the phrase in this way. Now, using a tape or your own voice, contrast the linked pronunciation with one in which each 't' is pronounced. Emphasize that the one 't' pronunciation is the way English people speak – it is not careless or sloppy. Suggest that they can pronounce this way too – they may certainly find it easier. A brief activity like this on a simple point of pronunciation will make learners aware that they should be on the look-out for ways in which English people actually speak and not rely too heavily on written forms.

Sound insertion

Exercises based on counting the number of sounds learners can hear are also useful for introducing the phenomenon of sound insertion.

Procedure

Present a selection of short phrases such as the following:

I'd like to own a car.

I can't see it.

These contain examples of sound insertion. In the first sentence speakers will link the vowels of 'to' and 'own' with a /w/ sound; in the second the vowels of 'see' and 'it' will be linked with a /j/ sound (see 2.2.4). Proceed as above, asking the class to count the number of sounds in each word, and then saying a phrase as a unit and counting the number of sounds in the phrase. Make sure the /j/ glide or the /w/ glide is used as appropriate. The class will probably come up with the same total for the words and for the phrase. If they don't hear the sound insertion, prompt them by pointing to the boundary between the words and asking them to listen very carefully. Contrast the natural pronunciation with one which separates the two vowels. You may also want to do some discrimination exercises, alternating the natural linked pronunciation with an unnatural unlinked pronunciation to see if they can hear the difference.

As part of these exercises it may be useful to introduce a notation for linkage. The most commonly used is a tie drawn between the final and initial sounds:

I want‿to

For sound insertion between vowels, a small 'y' or 'w' can be written within the tie:

to‿weat

Similar activities can be done in a purely oral/aural mode. One way of doing this is to prepare a tape recording of an English speaker pronouncing phrases both with the normal linkage and without. The pairs should be labelled (a) or (b). Play each pair to the learners, and then ask them which pronunciation is better. They should react with surprise or puzzlement at your asking them to evaluate what will probably sound to them like two equally good examples of English speech. If you do get this reaction, then ask them if they can hear any differences. Prompt with questions about separate words, pauses ('Does the speaker stop between words?'), and speed ('Does one phrase seem slower than the other?'). See if they can imitate the two contrasting pronunciations. When they begin to notice the differences, you can describe the linked pronunciation as more 'normal' or 'natural'. A chopping motion with the hands can be a useful way to describe the stop and start character of the unlinked pronunciation.

The purpose of these activities is to open learners' ears to the phenomenon of linkage, to introduce them to the idea that in English the words are connected up and that sounds sometimes disappear. They must depend on their ears to inform them about the sound of English – the written words can be misleading. Some learners will be more receptive to this notion than others. French speakers should be unperturbed because of the phenomenon of liaison in French; German and Chinese speakers will have more difficulty with linkage. It is not necessary to present explicit rules for the phenomenon at this stage. Some extension activities which involve working on the phonological rules will be discussed in Chapter 4.

**3.8
General awareness-building activities**

The previous sections have focused on activities which can be used to build awareness of specific aspects of English pronunciation (word stress, sentence stress, sounds, intonation, weak forms, connected speech simplifications and linkage). More general, non-specific, awareness-building activities can be useful in particular teaching situations. For example, the teacher may encounter a negative attitude towards matters of pronunciation on the part of some learners, and may feel that unless this is counter-balanced in some way then any attempts to improve pronunciation will have little chance of success. Or, if the learning experiences of the group have concentrated on reading and writing English, to the virtual exclusion of oral/aural work, then the teacher may feel that a general awareness activity may help in the transition to work on spoken English. In such circumstances, time devoted to the issue of pronunciation has value if it can simply put the forthcoming work into context, and help prepare the students by making them think about the task of making new sounds which is before them. Even in the absence of specific points of focus such as those mentioned above, time spent discussing the issue of pronunciation in a general way can help to stimulate interest, increase motivation, and (to borrow an expression from sport) 'gear up' the learners for pronunciation work. It can also give the teacher an opportunity to establish the respective teacher's and learner's role. The learner has the responsibility and right to choose how much time and effort to devote to this area; the teacher is a guide, a provider of models and feedback, and a language informant.

Here are two ways of organizing a discussion of pronunciation with groups of learners. The first is based on a questionnaire; the second centres on samples of the native languages of the learners spoken with a heavy foreign accent. Both aim to help learners develop a concern for the pronunciation of English through their personal experiences of language in use.

3.8.1
Questionnaire-based discussion

The following questions, or a selection from them, can be used to stimulate a discussion of the importance of 'good pronunciation'. The questions can be answered and discussed in class informally, or learners could complete a written questionnaire and then compare their answers in small groups or pairs before a whole-class discussion. Alternatively, if the teacher has used the questions with other groups or classes, the different sets of responses can be compared. All these possibilities have an information-gathering dimension to them (the last most clearly of all) and give the individual a chance to relate his or her responses to those of others. The questions and discussion can be carried out in the mother tongue in the case of monolingual classes. This may be necessary at the lower levels of proficiency in English, and may also be advisable at higher levels, to promote a meaningful discussion.

Questionnaire

1 Imagine you are talking in your own language with a foreigner. The person doesn't speak your language very well and is very difficult to understand. What do you do? Do you:
   (a) pretend you understand even when you don't?
   (b) ask him or her to repeat everything slowly and carefully?
   (c) try to get away?

2 What do you say when the foreign speaker apologizes for his poor accent? Do you:
   (a) tell him his accent is very good even when it isn't?
   (b) tell him that his poor accent doesn't matter?
   (c) tell him that his accent is very bad and that he must work hard to improve it?

3 How do you feel when a foreigner pronounces your name wrong?
   (a) very angry
   (b) it bothers me a little
   (c) it bothers me a lot
   (d) it doesn't bother me at all

4 How do you feel when you meet a foreigner who speaks your language with a very good accent?
   (a) surprised
   (b) pleased
   (c) not surprised
   (d) full of admiration
   (e) don't care or think about it

5 In the future, who will you speak English to?
   (a) mostly English people visiting my country who don't know my language
   (b) mostly English-speaking people in this country (Britain, USA, etc.)
   (c) mostly non-English people who don't know my language and whose language I don't know, so that we speak English together
   (d) don't know

6 Do you think it is more important to have good pronunciation when:
   (a) you are speaking English to English people?
   (b) you are speaking English to non-English people?

7 Below are some situations. When is it most important to pronounce well? Put them in order of importance with a number if you want.
   (a) speaking on the telephone
   (b) meeting someone for the first time
   (c) talking to someone you know very well (a good friend) in an informal situation (e.g. at a party)

(d) doing business in English (e.g. at the bank, post office, bus station, railway station, in shops, etc.)
(e) talking to strangers (e.g. asking the way)
(f) chatting to a fellow student (e.g. during break time)

These questions fall into two groups: questions 1–4 exploit learners' own experiences and 5–7 are concerned with the factors which determine the need for good pronunciation. Let's look at what points should emerge through these questions.

Through questions 1–4 the learners are guided towards realizations about the way they themselves react to foreign-accented speech. Such insights might help them to sympathize with English people who have to cope with the accented English they produce, and perhaps motivate them to greater effort in matters of pronunciation. Questions 1 and 2 may lead to quite specific insights about the behaviour of native English speakers: that sometimes praise is given out of kindness and a desire to encourage, rather than because it is deserved, and that native speakers can be reluctant to criticize or correct. If learners opt for answer (c) in response to question 1 this may even lead them to a possible explanation for any coldness or unwillingness to converse on the part of English people that they may encounter or have encountered (the English person may simply be trying to escape from what is a difficult or tedious conversation). The realization that people may be more eager to talk with them if they are *easy* to talk with, may help to increase the learners' motivation to pronounce well. (Of course the teacher can make these points even if no student has chosen the relevant answer.)

Questions 5–7 ask the learners to consider the roles that situation, setting, and listener play in the use of spoken language. Questions 5 and 6 concern the listener. When the listener is himself a non-native speaker, then he will tend to be more tolerant in matters of pronunciation. On the other hand, native speakers, especially if they are not used to conversing with foreigners, may have a much lower level of tolerance. Through discussion and a comparison of their answers to question 5, learners should realize that, depending on their probable present and future language needs, *they* can decide how much importance they will give to pronunciation, although they must keep revising this assessment in the light of the reactions from others, including the teacher. The teacher can guide and provide, they themselves can select and give priority. Question 7 focuses on the role of setting and situation as well as the participants. Learners need to realize that in some situations they don't need to worry too much about their pronunciation. If they are talking to a close friend, or even just someone they know is interested in them as a person (at, for example, a party), then they can be sure that he or she will be quite tolerant of mispronunciations, that there is no urgency about the messages that are exchanged. Indeed, more often than not, party chat is language which is low on content and serves to cement social relationships simply through the exchange of words. In this context, accuracy is relatively unimportant and the listener usually displays a great deal of patience. However, if a learner is carrying out a transaction in a bank, and there is a long queue, it is very important to pronounce well in order to avoid causing irritation and frustration. This realization, that there is a degree of flexibility in matters of pronunciation, may help learners whose performance is harmed by over-anxiety to pronounce well *all the time*, and relaxation may actually lead to better performance.

<table>
<tr><td>

3.8.2
A tape-based
activity

</td><td>

A tape recording of poorly accented and unintelligible speech in a foreign language by a native English speaker can also serve as the focus for a general awareness-building activity. Such a tape recording is a very direct way to stimulate discussion of the implications for communication and social interaction of heavily foreign-accented speech. Even if the class does not share one native language, a tape recording of one of the native languages can be used to start off the discussion with one section of the class, and then the others can contribute their reactions to foreigners speaking their respective languages.

</td></tr>
</table>

Procedure
Play the tape you have prepared, introducing it with a question such as: 'I'd like to know what you think about this speaker?' Then elicit student reactions with questions similar to 1–3 above:

1 How would you describe this person's accent?
2 Would you like having a conversation with this speaker?
3 Do you dislike hearing your language spoken in this way?
4 Why do you think the person pronounces so badly/in this way?
   (a) the person doesn't really care about pronunciation
   (b) the person hasn't been told how bad their accent is
   (c) it's very difficult to pronounce this language well
   (d) the person hasn't been taught about pronunciation

The group may also be able to identify words which are very important and need to be pronounced well (such as names, or basic words which might cause confusion with other words if badly pronounced), or words which are slightly mispronounced but are nevertheless easily intelligible. If the discussion does take this direction, the points made can be related to the notion of relative importance.

Activities such as these are beneficial to both teacher and learners. The teacher can get a general idea of how responsive the learners are likely to be to pronunciation work, both as a group and as individuals. Adamant claims by an individual that he or she doesn't mind how foreigners pronounce his or her native language may correlate with a lack of concern for his or her own pronunciation in English. Some learners may demonstrate very high levels of concern, and, if their speech is very unfluent, or if they are not eager to speak at all, this may identify them as over-anxious to the point of debilitation. These learners may need to be encouraged to relax a bit more. The learners may be helped to understand and interpret the reactions of English speakers to them, to consider the options available to them and the implications of these for their own use of English. A higher level of awareness and concern usually has a positive effect on motivation and therefore achievement.

References

1 This technique was developed from a discussion with Helen Oatey.

2 I am grateful to A. Underhill, International House, Hastings for this suggestion.

3 The two example dialogues have been adapted from dialogues in C. Mortimer *Stress Time* (Cambridge University Press 1976).

4 These examples were taken from J. Abbot *Meet the Press* (Cambridge University Press 1981), which is a good source of headlines.

5 See Chapter 10 in P. Ladefoged *A Course in Phonetics* (Harcourt, Brace, Jovanovich 1975).

6 A good source for ambiguous dialogues is A. Maley and A. Duff *Variations on a Theme* (Cambridge University Press 1978).

7 Good sources of minimal pairs are: J. Trim *English Pronunciation Illustrated* (Cambridge University Press 1975) and A. Baker *Ship or Sheep?* and *Tree or Three?* (Cambridge University Press 1981 and 1982).

8 D. B. Pisoni et al 'Identification and Discrimination of a New Linguistic Contrast' (*Research on Speech Perception – Progress Report* 4 Indiana University 1978).

9 R. Campbell and B. Dodd 'Hearing by Eye' (*Quarterly Journal of Experimental Psychology* 32 1980).

10 J. and M. Trim *Phonetic Bingo* (Cambridge University Press 1978).

4

Extending and consolidating

4.1
Word stress

In Chapter 3, section 3, we looked at some simple ways of introducing the notion of word stress to learners. In this section we will look at some further activities which will involve the learners in more detailed discoveries about the way it operates in English. As we saw, word stress in English is variable – any syllable of a polysyllabic word can carry the main stress. This is very different from other languages which have 'fixed' word stress (that is, in a two-syllable word, the second syllable will always be stressed; in a three-syllable word the final syllable will always be stressed, and so on). Indeed, in some languages the stress is always on the root, no matter what affixes are added. If either of these tendencies are present in their own language, learners of English will unconsciously assume that English has a similar regularity.

As well as being variable, English word stress is also *mobile*. In 'economy', the stress falls on the second syllable (ec<u>o</u>nomy), but in 'economic', it falls on the third syllable or, counting from the end of the word, the 'next-to-last' or 'penultimate' syllable (econ<u>o</u>mic). Having become familiar with the pronunciation of one form of a word, learners will (quite logically!) assume that the stress stays on the same syllable in other forms of the word, or, to express it in another way, they will assume that prefixes and suffixes make no difference to the placement of the stress. But in English words they do.

4.1.1
Working on word
stress patterns

The exercises outlined in section 1 of Chapter 3 can be used to make learners aware that English word stress is variable and that they therefore need to pay attention to the location of the main stress when they come across a new word.

Stress mobility

As soon as learners begin to encounter related forms of a word, then this is the opportune time to do some exploratory activities on the *mobility* of English word stress.

Procedure

A few pairs, or triplets, of related words can be used to illustrate the phenomenon. For example, if the students have encountered *photography*, *photographer*, and *photograph* in a text, the teacher should emphasize the differences in the placement of the main stress. The three words can be put into columns according to their form class (noun, verb, adjective, etc.). Or, a more immediately accessible and meaningful classification might be something like the following:

name of activity	person who does it	object involved
photography	photographer	photograph
advertising	advertiser	advertisement
librarianship	librarian	library

The stress can then be indicated for each word in the set.

After the teacher has presented a few examples of sets of related words, the learners can be asked to try to think up more examples. The teacher can speed up this task by providing one item from a set and asking them to fill in the other columns. (This has the added advantage of increasing familiarity with certain suffixes in English and can be a good lesson on the productivity of these suffixes.) Or the list can be kept as an 'open file' and added to whenever students encounter similar sets of words.

4.1.2.
Using rules for stress placement

Although at first glance the placement of word stress seems totally unpredictable as well as highly variable, there *are* rules and patterns. Certain suffixes seem to determine or 'govern' where the stress falls in a word. If students can be made aware of these patterns, then they will be able to figure out the stress pattern of a new word for themselves. Of course, the rules can just be presented to the learners; some teaching materials have taken this approach. But another strategy is to get the learners to discover the rules for themselves. The chances of remembering a rule seem to be far greater if you have been involved in the discovery of that rule, if you have 'cracked the system' yourself.

Discovering the rules

(A brief summary of word stress rules appears at the end of this section.)

Procedure

Select a set of endings which govern word stress placement. Choose three or four, for example: '-ic', '-tion', and '-ical'. Prepare sets of cards with a single word written on each and the stressed syllable marked in some way. It is also a good idea to indicate syllable divisions. Mix up the cards and give a set of about twenty to thirty to small groups or pairs of students. Make sure each group has a good number of examples of each suffix-determined pattern. Tell the learners to spread out the cards and divide them into groups, according to the number of syllables. Then ask them to do a further grouping according to which syllable in the word is stressed, counting from the end of the word. You will probably need to illustrate the principle of counting syllables from the end of the word.

At this stage the teacher circulates and asks what words are in the

groups and whether they can see any patterns. Use prompts such as:
— In the words you have with '- ic' at the end, which syllable is stressed?
— Does it matter how many syllables the word has?
— Do all the words ending in '-ic' have the stress in the same place?

If you think the groups will need more guidance in the task, the cards can be prepared with the endings underlined, or coloured in different ink, to draw their attention to what is going on.

As the learners discover the rules, a formula can be devised for each. One way to do this is to use the small and large circle notation and the suffix, thus:

o o O -ic (*example*: 'economic')
o O -ion (*example*: 'inflation')

4.1.3
Levels of stress

When working on words of three, four or more syllables, the teacher and the learners may notice that the two-way distinction between stress and unstress seems to be breaking down. It may seem that there are not just two levels of stress ('primary' and 'secondary') but three ('primary', 'secondary' and 'tertiary'). For example, if you say the word 'magnification' it may seem that instead of

o o o O o
mag ni fi ca tion

the strongest stress is on '-ca-', there is a slightly weaker one on 'mag-' and three weak stresses on '-ni-', '-fi-', and '-tion', thus:

o . . O .
mag ni fi ca tion

But it is only when the word is said in *isolation* that we seem to hear three levels of stress. When said as part of a sentence, such as: 'The magnification has been increased', we tend to hear only two levels of stress (stress on '-ca-' and unstress on the other four syllables). In fact, if you say this sentence with the 'o . . O .' pattern on 'magnification' it sounds as if you are correcting someone who has just said something like: 'The clarification has been increased.'

There are groups of English words which *seem* to have three levels of stress. For example, 'regular' has the pattern 'Ooo', but 'regulate' seems to have a 'secondary stress' on the last syllable:

O . o
reg u late

The same applies to the following pairs of words:

O . o	O o o
criticize	critical
optimize	optimal
multiply	multiple
circulate	circular
minimize	minimal

Notice that in the first column of words on page 61 there is a full vowel in the last syllable of each of the words, whereas the words in the second column have a weak or 'reduced' vowel in the last syllable. We seem to hear a secondary stress in the words in the first column *because* of the presence of a full vowel. The same thing happens with 'explanation' and 'explanatory'. If you say 'explanation' with a full vowel /ɛ/ as in 'b*e*d' in the first syllable, you will probably hear the stress pattern as:

o · O ·
ex pla na tion

with secondary stress on 'ex-' and tertiary stress on '-pla-' and '-tion'. But if you say 'explanation' with the reduced vowel 'schwa' in the first syllable, you will not hear a secondary stress on the 'ex-':

o o O o
ex pla na tion

So, in summary, three levels of stress can sometimes be heard in long English words, but this seems to happen only when: (1) the word is said in isolation; (2) the word is in a position in a sentence where it is very strongly stressed; or (3) full vowels are used.

To deal with these three situations a three-level system can be used and an appropriate notation for marking the levels, such as the one we have used above. But it is advisable to wait for the students themselves to notice the possibility of a three-level system, rather than introducing it to them. There is no point in overloading them and risking feelings of confusion and frustration. Indeed, a two-level distinction is perfectly adequate and the phonetic evidence does seem to indicate that syllables are simply stressed or unstressed.[1]

4.1.4
Exercises for
hearing stress

If the students seem to need more work on identifying stress and unstress, then some perceptual exercises like those used for consonants and vowels can be done.

Same or different?

The learners are presented with words or short phrases in pairs, and asked to say whether they are the same or different in stress pattern. For example:

operate	beautiful
milk and sugar	tea and coffee
coca-cola	lemonade

Odd One Out?

Give a list of words or short phrases. Learners have to spot the pattern which is different from the others:

at dinner   the paper   potato   not enough   forever   a teaspoon

Matching exercise

Learners are given sets of cards with words or phrases and a set of cards with a stress pattern. They must find words which match the pattern.

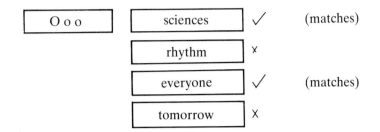

Or, a model word or phrase can be used instead of a pattern card.

If done in pairs or groups, these activities can stimulate a lot of discussion and experimentation with different versions, and are conducive to greater awareness and familiarity with stress pattern.

A summary of English word stress rules

Rule 1

'Front weight' in nouns and adjectives. There seems to be a very strong tendency in English for what is called core vocabulary to have stress on the first syllable. This means that many common nouns and adjectives will have stress on the first syllable.

Examples:

water	people	brother	table
finger	woman	sister	ugly
father	butter	pretty	apple
mother			

Rule 2

Two- and three-syllable words which have a prefix. In words with prefixes such as 'be-', 'in-', 'dis-', 'ex-', 'un-', etc., the stress is almost always on the second or third syllable, i.e. prefixes are not stressed in English words. Note that the majority of these words are verbs.

Examples:

repeat	begin	because	distrust
increase	exhaust	infer	inspect
conclude	confer	invite	understand

Rule 3

Words with suffixes. If we examine English words with suffixes, a similar tendency is revealed: suffixes are never stressed.

Examples:

-ly	quietly
-al	original
-ive	administrative
-ent/ant	equivalent
-ic	automatic

Another general tendency is for the stressed syllable to be somewhere in the middle of the word, rather than on the first or last syllable in words of four, five, or six syllables.

Rule 3.1

Certain suffixes determine on which of the other syllables the stress will fall. There are very many suffixes which cause the syllable *before the suffix* to be stressed. These are:

-ive (impressive)	-iate (deviate)
-ient (incipient)	-iary (pecuniary)
-iant (deviant)	-iable (negotiable)
-ial (substantial)	-ish (diminish)
-ion (invention)	-ify (identify)
-ic (geographic)	-ium (premium)
-ian (median)	-ior (superior)
-ious (infectious)	-io (radio)
-ical (economical)	-iar (familiar)
-ity (opportunity)	-ible (impossible)

It doesn't matter if the stress was on a different syllable in the form of the word without the suffix (sometimes called the 'base' word); the stress will move from wherever it was to the syllable before the suffix when any of these suffixes are added.

Rule 3.2

The suffix '-able' usually does not change the stress pattern of a word to which it is added. So in 'commend' the stress is on the second syllable, in 'commendable' it remains on the second syllable.

Examples:

adapt	adaptable
rely	reliable
knowledge	knowledgeable
detest	detestable

Exceptions:

demonstrate	demonstrable
admire	admirable
prefer	preferable

Rule 3.3

The following suffixes cause the stress to be placed on the fourth syllable from the end of the word (this applies, of course, only to words of four or more syllables):

-ary (vocabulary)
-ator (investigator)
-mony (alimony)
-acy (intimacy)
-ory (category)

Rule 4

Compound words. There are also some rules for determining stress in compound words. These are words which are formed by combining two nouns, a noun and an adjective, a verb and a preposition, etc. It is very common for compound words which are nouns to have stress on the first element. So, the tendency in Rule 1 also applies to compound nouns.

Examples:

a teapot	a chairman	a put-on	a crossword
a windscreen	a postman	a pushover	a hotdog
a newspaper	a walkout	a grandfather	a blackbird

Rule 4.1

Some compound words are formed from an adjective plus a noun. When the same two words are used separately in a sentence, each word will have equal or independent stress. For example, compare:

What a beautiful <u>blackbird</u>!
Look at that big <u>black</u> <u>bird</u>!

Rule 5

There is a set of *words which can be used as either a verb or a noun* in English (there are a few cases of noun or adjective):

increase	export	import	content
overflow	insult	decrease	

In all these words, the noun has the stress on the first syllable, and the verb has the stress on the last syllable. This seems to fit with Rules 1 and 2: the nouns will have front weighting and the verbs, with a prefix as the first syllable, will have stress on the second syllable.

4.2
Using stress in sentences

In Chapter 3 we looked at some ways of introducing learners to the way a speaker gives the listener information about the relative importance of different parts of a message. Here we will look at ways of exploring the use of stress in sentences to convey specific meanings.

4.2.1
Asserting, denying, correcting

Conversations are full of negotiation. Speakers often want to assert a fact or opinion quite strongly, deny what another speaker has said and offer a correction, or ask about alternatives and options in order to come to an agreement about what to do. English has various means of carrying out these functions, including special constructions and vocabulary such as 'it's me who has to tell him' (the cleft formation) or 'on the contrary'. However, English speakers very often resort to stress to achieve their ends. For example, if a speaker has just made a statement with which you disagree, then you can assert the opposite by repeating their words almost exactly, but changing the verb from positive to negative or vice versa, and moving the main sentence stress:

<u>People</u> are <u>funny</u>.
People <u>aren't</u> funny. They're <u>strange</u>.

Learners of English need to be aware of this use of stress in order to follow discussions, arguments, and exchanges of opinions. The ability to use stress in this way is also a useful speaking skill. Below are two suggestions for working on the use of stress to assert, deny, and correct. The first set of activities uses short two-part exchanges in which one speaker makes a statement, part of which is inaccurate. The other speaker draws attention to the mistake and corrects it by placing very strong stress on the relevant item.

Correct me if I'm wrong[2]

Procedure

Write up on the board a date, time of day, the price of something, some measurement, or the result of a calculation, in the following way:

No, (it's) —————.

(*For example*: No, it's Tuesday, May 23rd.)

Tell the learners that they must respond to any questions you ask only with these words. Then ask questions in which one point only is wrong, such as: 'Are we leaving on June 23rd?'; 'Is today May 24th?'; 'Is it the 21st today?' In responding, the students should place very strong stress on the item that has to be corrected, for example: 'No, it's Tuesday, May twenty-third.' The items which the questioner has got correct should not receive much stress at all. If the learners do not place stress appropriately, the teacher can present a model, and if necessary give a brief explanation of the force and function of this use of stress. The term *contrastive stress*, which is often used in teaching materials and workbooks, can be introduced, but *correcting stress* is also a useful term, and perhaps more immediately understandable.

After some practice with the teacher as questioner, students can be grouped into pairs. Slips of paper or cards can be prepared with a variety of responses. Some may be linked to particular contexts such as travelling by air (airport departure gates, flight numbers, flight arrivals/departures, etc.), as in the example below:

No, they're landing at Gatwick.
No, it's Gate number 12.
No, it's Flight 257 for Rome.

Both learners examine the set response, then one learner must think up a question with an inaccuracy. The other gives the response with appropriate stress. Then they can swap roles. The sentence frame can be varied slightly by the introduction of such words as 'actually', 'well', 'I think it's ————— '. The restricted language and provision of cues makes this activity suitable for lower proficiency levels. For more advanced levels a role play task can be designed which will put one student into the role of 'corrector'. The following activity is based on a psychodrama technique known as 'shadowing'.

A role play – 'Spokesman and aide'

The situation centres on a spokesman or representative of a company, government/government agency, etc., who is briefing members of the press on recent developments or the outcome of negotiations. This spokesman is assisted by an aide who is an expert in the particular field. The aide has more accurate information than the spokesman, who may actually be merely a mouthpiece for the government or institution. The aide has the background knowledge and expertise to be able to correct any inaccuracies in the facts given by the spokesman, or modify/qualify the terms used in particular statements.

Procedure
The learners are chosen to take the roles of 'spokesman' and 'aide'. The rest of the class listen to their presentation. Spokesman and aide each receive a set of cue cards which contain the information to be presented. But in some instances the aide's cards have slightly different information to the spokesman's. Using the cue cards, the spokesman makes his or her presentation. The aide sits beside him or her, and whenever the aide notices a difference between the cue card information and what the spokesman is saying, he or she must interrupt politely and diplomatically correct the incorrect point. (The assumption is that the aide's information is always more reliable.) Some rehearsal of appropriate forms to do this may be needed. The 'presentation' should shape up in the following way:

SPOKESMAN: We are closing down three of our factories.
AIDE: Excuse me, but it's only <u>two</u> factories.
SPOKESMAN: This will mean the loss of 500 jobs.
AIDE: In actual fact, we think about <u>700</u> jobs will be lost.

Cue cards for this example would contain this information:

Spokesman	*Aide*
factories closing 3	factories closing 2
jobs lost 500	jobs lost 700

Other members of the class can become more involved by asking questions and requesting clarification of particular points from the spokesman.

This is a fairly demanding activity and can occupy a substantial part of a lesson. The language involved is fairly open-ended. Cue cards can be designed to suit the level of the learners, and also to provide some indication of grammatical structures and vocabulary if needed. The activity offers practice in a variety of speaking skills (providing information in a fairly structured way, interrupting politely, making corrections, etc.) which are all valuable to learners. However, the point of focus for teacher *monitoring* and *correction* should be the use of contrastive stress. In order to make this an activity which focuses on pronunciation, the teacher should restrict correction and evaluative comments to the use of stress.

4.2.2
Questioning
alternatives

Another way in which English speakers exploit stress is in questioning another person about alternatives, possibilities, or options. Often the situation is one in which one speaker has some information and wants to check if his or her recall of that information is accurate: 'Was it _____ who said that?' The following activity incorporates the essentials of such situations in a matching task format. The activity is based on short narratives involving at least two characters and a set of actions or events.

It is essential that the characters could equally feasibly carry out the actions mentioned in the story. Here is a story that meets these criteria.

A Roman folk-tale

Once there were a king and a queen. The king had a storeroom of honey. One of the servants loved honey. He made a key to the storeroom and began to steal the honey. The queen thought up a clever plan to find the thief. She called together all the servants. She accused them of stealing the honey. But the servants all denied the theft. Then the queen suddenly said: 'You cannot deny your guilt – I can see honey in your beard.' The guilty servant was frightened and he raised his hand to wipe his beard. The queen knew he must be the thief.

Procedure

A cue sheet is prepared in which the characters are separated from their actions and these are presented as halves of sentences in two columns, one for the characters, one for the actions/events:

the queen	called together all the servants
one of the servants	quickly raised his hand to wipe his beard
the guilty servant	had a storeroom full of honey
the servants	denied stealing the honey
the king	knew which servant was the thief
	loved honey
	accused the servants of the theft
	thought up a clever plan to find the thief
	made a key to the storeroom and began to steal the honey
	said suddenly, 'You cannot deny your guilt – I can see honey in your beard.'

Note that the order of events and actions is changed – the first character and event are not the first to occur in the story.

 Students are divided into pairs: one student (A) receives the original narrative, the other (B) receives the list. B must reconstruct the narrative by asking student A whether character _____ did action _____ or not. Most native speakers will use the cleft formation to do this, at least some of the time, for example: 'Was it _____ who _____ ?' Learners can be given this pattern to follow: the noun or noun phrase which follows the word 'it' in the structure will receive very strong stress, particularly when it is a second or third choice, for example: 'Was it the _____ who _____ ? No. Well, was it the _____ who _____ ?' The focus of teacher monitoring should be on this use of stress. If learners don't use it appropriately the teacher can give a model (a few examples on tape of native English speakers doing this can be useful for demonstration purposes). To help in the reconstruction of the story, lines can be drawn between characters and actions as these are discovered.

This activity also happens to be quite useful for the development of reading skills. The student who has the full text must repeatedly scan that text to check whether the questioner has hit upon an actual combination from the story. This is excellent practice in the skills of scanning a text for specific points of information. The questioner must also 'read for meaning' by reading through the lists for what look like feasible combinations. A strategy which works through the list mechanically will probably have slower results than one which is based on possible story frames and likely events.

4.3
Making sounds

Many learners will be able to produce new sounds simply by imitating what they hear, but if students seem to be unable to imitate then the teacher can help by giving directions. The teacher doesn't need to be an expert phonetician to do this. If teachers have some basic knowledge and a sensitivity to what is happening when they themselves make a particular sound, then they can give guidance and hints to learners which may help them to achieve the sound. In order to produce a particular sound, the vocal organs must assume quite a complex set of postures and carry out a set of precisely ordered movements. Timing and coordination of these must be very accurate. For some sounds it's fairly easy to sense what the vocal organs are doing; for others it is very difficult. Obviously, the only useful instructions to learners are ones that can be followed, responded to, understood and carried out, and controlled. 'Rest the tip of your tongue just behind your front teeth', is a fairly straightforward direction. However, 'Move your tongue forward about one millimetre closer to the roof of your mouth' is virtually impossible to follow, especially since the person may not even be able to figure out where the tongue is in the first place! Yet both these instructions might feasibly represent what is needed to produce a particular sound. Teachers should always remember that receiving directions about what to do with the vocal organs is completely alien to people. It is not how we learn to make the sounds of our native languages. This teaching strategy is very limited, and may fail completely with some very anxious and self-conscious learners. The English humorist J. K. Jerome described in *Three Men on the Bummel*, with great wit and sarcasm, the way *not* to give instructions. The following passage from the book on the agonies of an English person trying to learn how to pronounce certain German sounds can serve as a vivid reminder to teachers:

> I . . . think the pronunciation of a foreign tongue could be better taught than by demanding from the pupil those internal acrobatic feats that are generally impossible and always useless. This is the sort of instruction one receives. "Press your tonsils against the underside of your larynx. Then with the convex part of the septum curved upwards so as almost but not quite to touch the uvula, try with the tip of your tongue to reach your thyroid. Take a deep breath and compress your glottis. Now, without opening your lips, say 'Garoo'". And when you have done it they are not satisfied.[3]

4.3.1
Some
preliminaries

Here is a brief list of the postures and movements that people generally seem to find fairly easy to notice and control:

— lip position: whether the lips are pursed (as in whistling) or spread (as in a smile) or wide apart (as when yawning)

— contact (or close proximity) between the tongue and teeth: whether the sides of the tongue are touching the upper back teeth (the molars) or whether the tip of the tongue is touching the top or bottom front teeth

— contact (or close proximity) between the tongue and the roof of the mouth: whether the tip of the tongue is touching a part of the roof of the mouth, or whether the back of the tongue is.

It is usually very difficult for a person to feel whether the middle of the tongue is touching the roof of the mouth, or to tell which *part* of the roof is coming into contact with the tongue. Indeed, unless one is given some information about the areas of the roof of the mouth and how they can be named, it is very difficult to respond to any directions about contact with a particular area of the roof of the mouth.

Useful vocabulary

The teacher should check that the learners know the following names of the vocal organs:

lips – top and bottom or upper and lower
teeth – top and bottom or upper and lower, front teeth and back teeth
tongue – tip or front, back of the tongue and sides of the tongue

The following words will also be needed:

put/place
near   touching   close to
round   spread

4.3.2
Points to
remember

No sound is an island

Avoid demonstrating or asking learners to produce sounds in isolation. Sounds occur in syllables, surrounded by other sounds, so give the learners a real word or a nonsense word (preferably one that has no other sounds that are difficult for them). It certainly makes no sense to practise consonant sounds in isolation – the only consonant sound in English which occurs by itself is the /ʃ/ sound as in 'sh*oe*', used as a command to 'speak softly' or 'be quiet'. It's actually impossible to pronounce some sounds by themselves. If, for example, you try to make a /p/ or /t/ in isolation, what you end up doing is simply sustaining the 'start position' of these sounds. It makes more sense to make vowel sounds in isolation, because there are some words which are composed only of a vowel sound ('oh' and 'I'). But it must be remembered that sounds are influenced by, and influence, the other sounds around them. The /k/ in 'cool' is made slightly differently to the /k/ in 'cup'.[4] The learner must be able to produce sounds in many different positions and surroundings. The more practice he or she gets in doing this the better.

Position of sounds

It is usually easier for learners to produce a new sound in initial position. So start out with words where the sound is at the beginning of the word, then move on to words where it occurs at the end (which is slightly more difficult), then to middle position, and finally in combination with other sounds.

Self-correction

When a learner spontaneously corrects a sound or makes an adjustment, draw attention to the fact that they have done this by saying something like: 'Do you realize that you just put that sound right yourself?' It's important that learners realize that they are able to monitor their own speech and make adjustments without the teacher's interference.

Self-assessment

Likewise, when a learner is practising or attempting to make a sound for your comment, make sure you ask them for their judgement sometimes before providing your own assessment.[5]

4.3.3
Correction
techniques for
particular
difficulties

In Part Two correction techniques and teaching strategies are given for language-specific problems. In this section we will give some teaching strategies for problems which are shared by many learner groups and are therefore of general usefulness.

Difficulties with vowels (monothongs)

If a learner is having difficulty in producing one of the English vowels of the group /i/ as in 'beat', /ɪ/ as in 'bit', /ɛ/ as in 'bed' or /a/ as in 'hat', then this may be because the tongue is in the wrong position, either too close or too far away from the roof of the mouth. For example, if the student is trying to produce /ɛ/ as in 'ten', and the attempt sounds closer to /a/ as in 'tan', this is probably because the tongue is too far away from the roof of the mouth and needs to be brought closer. One way to help the student do this is to use a vowel with a closer tongue position that the student *can* produce. This vowel can be used as a kind of counterweight or counterbalance to the student's incorrect sound. So, if the student's attempt at /ɛ/ as in 'ten' sounds too much like /a/ as in 'tan', ask the student to make /ɪ/ as in 'tin' or /i/ as in 'teen'. Then instruct the student to alternate the two extremes (in this case the vowel in 'tan' and the one in 'tin' or 'teen'). The next step is for the student to try to glide very smoothly and slowly from one extreme to the other. At approximately the midpoint of the glide the student will, inevitably, produce the desired vowel. Try to get him or her to notice this. The diagram below indicates the relationship between this set of four vowels in terms of distance of the tongue from the roof of the mouth:

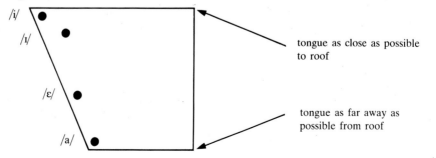

tongue as close as possible to roof

tongue as far away as possible from roof

Here is another example. If the learner can produce /i/ as in 'sh*ee*p' but not /ɪ/ as in 'h*i*t', then schwa can be used as the counterweight. Ask the student to alternate schwa and /i/ and then to say /i/ and glide slowly towards the schwa vowel. At some point along the glide, the /ɪ/ vowel as in 'h*i*t' will be produced.

This technique has been called the *see-saw technique*. It can be very effective in helping learners to get a sense of where a particular vowel is produced. This technique can be effective for several groups of vowels. The following diagram shows which vowels can be used as counterweights for other vowels:

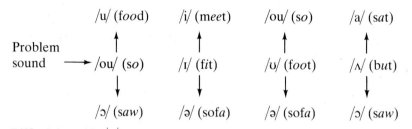

Problem sound ⟶

/u/ (f*oo*d)	/i/ (m*ee*t)	/ou/ (s*o*)	/a/ (s*a*t)
↑	↑	↑	↑
/ou/ (s*o*)	/ɪ/ (f*i*t)	/ʊ/ (f*oo*t)	/ʌ/ (b*u*t)
↓	↓	↓	↓
/ɔ/ (s*aw*)	/ə/ (sof*a*)	/ə/ (sof*a*)	/ɔ/ (s*aw*)

Difficulties with /h/

The /h/ sound in English, as in 'h*eat*', 'h*at*', 'h*ot*', is not a single sound. It can be produced in many different positions. This can be easily demonstrated by saying each of the above words – the position for making /h/ is different in each one. /h/ is simply a period of breath before a vowel. If a learner has difficulty in making /h/ ask him or her to whisper a sequence of vowels (reciting the vowel letters in the alphabet will do). The learner will invariably produce all kinds of /h/. This should help learners to get used to how it feels to make /h/.

If the learner is making a sound that has too much of a 'hissing quality', then point out that /h/ is a very light sound and that very little force or breath is required to make it. A lightweight piece of paper held in front of the lips should not flutter at all when /h/ is made properly.

Some learners may use /h/ too much. This problem is aggravated by (and has its source in) English spelling conventions. If the learner is pronouncing 'h' where there should be none, for example if 'arm' is pronounced to sound like 'harm' then it may help to draw the learner's attention to the fact that there *is* a sound before the vowel, but it is not 'h'. In English, words that begin with a vowel often have what is called a glottal stop[6] before the vowel. This sound is very much like a quick cough or 'catch' in the throat. The vowel seems to begin very abruptly because of this preceding glottal stop. Demonstrate this to the learners, and ask them to try to concentrate on giving words with an initial vowel a very sharp, abrupt start. This may help them to eliminate unwanted h's from their speech.

Difficulties with aspiration of /p, t, k/

When these sounds are made there is a very slight pause before the following vowel, during which a slight puff of air is released. This puff of air is very characteristic of the way these sounds are made in English and is called *aspiration*. /b, d, and g/ do not have any such aspiration. It is vital that learners use appropriate aspiration when they pronounce '*p*it, *t*ip, and *k*it'. If there is no obvious puff of air, then English listeners will probably hear these sounds as /b, d, g/ respectively.

One technique is to tell the learners to sound an /h/ immediately after these three sounds when they pronounce them. It can be especially helpful to do some practice exercises using words beginning with 'h' as help-words for other words beginning with initial /p, t, k/. For example, for 'part', 'heart' can be a help word. To pronounce 'part', tell the learners to make /p/ and then say 'heart'. This should result in the word 'part' with adequate aspiration. Similarly, 'hill' can be used for 'till'; 'hat' for 'cat'; 'heat' for 'Pete', etc. After a few examples and demonstrations, learners can be advised to 'think of adding an 'h' after /p, t, k/'. (Of course, this technique is not useful for learners for whom 'h' itself is a problem sound!)

The teacher can also demonstrate the presence of a puff of air by holding a lighted match or a thin piece of paper in front of the mouth as words beginning with /p, t, k/ are said. The match should flicker or the paper move when these words are pronounced, proof that there is a strong puff of air.

Note: /p, t, k/ are not aspirated when they occur after another consonant, for example in '*s*peak, *s*top, *s*kate' there is no aspiration. Aspiration is a feature of these sounds only in word or syllable initial position.

Difficulties with /r/

As we saw in the section on Sounds and Symbols, there are many varieties of /r/ in English accents, and because of English speakers' familiarity with the range of types, many learners will be able to use /r/ of their native language when speaking English and be perfectly intelligible.

If learners do want to use the almost vowel-like 'gliding' sound characteristic of British RP, many southern English accents, and some American accents, then here are some instructions for its production. Each of these suggestions uses another sound as a starting point or help-sound, so they will only be usable if the learner can make that sound.

/a/

1 Tell the learner to make /a/ as in '*c*a*t*' and, as they do, to curve the tip of the tongue slightly upwards.

2 Make sure that the tongue tip doesn't touch the roof of the mouth.

/j/ as in 'yes' or /i/ as in '*eat*'

These are useful sounds for learners who tend to use a trilled or rolled /r/ in the mother tongue (Italian, Spanish, Arabic). For both /j/ and /i/ the sides of the tongue are held tightly against the upper back teeth, as for the target sound /r/. This inhibits a trilling action of the tongue tip.

1 Get ready to pronounce /j/ (or /i/).

2 As you make the sound, curl the tip of the tongue slightly upwards.

3 Don't move the sides of your tongue or touch the tip against the roof of the mouth.

/ʒ/ as in 'rou*ge*'

This is a useful helping sound for learners who tend to use a 'back' /r/ (French, German).

1 Select some words in which /r/ follows another consonant, for example 'bread, dry, grey', etc.

2 Tell the learners to substitute the sound /ʒ/ for /r/ in these words.

3 Tell them to try to feel where the tongue is when they do this. This is the position it must be in for /r/ (i.e. in the middle of the mouth).

4 Tell them to shorten the sound and make it 'smoother'. The result should be quite close to /r/.

Some learners cannot perceive the difference between English /r/ and other sounds, in particular /l/ and /n/, and will mix them up in production. It helps to make learners aware of the differences between the sounds:

1 Emphasize that for /r/ the tip of the tongue never touches the roof of the mouth – for both /l/ and /n/ it must touch the roof of the mouth. A simple diagram can be useful:

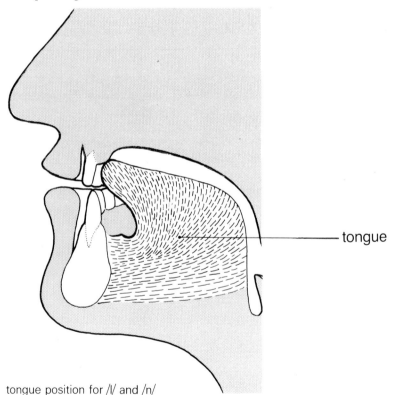

tongue

tongue position for /l/ and /n/

2 Point out that English speakers often purse the lips slightly when making /r/ (although /r/ can be made without doing this). If they try to imitate this lip position when they make the sound, it may help them to establish two sounds.

Difficulties with the 'th' sounds – /θ/ (*th*ink) and /ð/ (*th*at)

These are new sounds for many learners. A suggestion often given is to ask learners to make an exaggerated version of the sounds, for example:

1 Tell the learner to place the tip of the tongue between the upper and lower front teeth, or to gently bite the tip of the tongue.

2 Push the air through trying to make a hissing sound – this will result in /θ/ as in '*th*in'.

3 For /ð/ as in '*th*at' tell the learners to push the air through making a 'buzzing' noise (for 'voicing').

This often works, but many learners may react negatively, especially if they notice that native speakers don't show their tongue when making the 'th' sounds, and such learners may well decide that 'the business of sticking a section of pink tongue between the teeth is strictly a matter for teacher'.[7] The following comment by a French learner is revealing: 'Les 'th' ça fait postillonner. On coince la langue dans les dents, c'est vachement compliqué.' (The 'th' sound makes you spit and splutter. You have to stick your tongue in your teeth, it's not easy.)

If learners seem self-conscious or resistant, then try the 'chewing gum technique':

1 Give each learner a small piece of gum.

2 After a few moments of communal chewing tell them to press the gum up against the back of the upper front teeth.

3 Then tell them to touch the tongue lightly at the bottom edge of the gum, and force the air through.

The novelty of the gum technique can make the required tongue position for 'th' memorable. It provides an artificial aid for familiarizing learners with the necessary posture for the sound.

Learners who substitute /s/, /z/, /t/, /d/ for 'th' may be helped by being told to position the gum on the roof of the mouth immediately behind the upper front teeth; for /s/, /z/, /t/, and /d/ they must touch the gum; for 'th' they must avoid it.

Some learners may be able to make the 'th' sounds 'on demand' but when speaking spontaneously some or all of them are 'lost'. One strategy is to tell learners to pause before any noun, adjective, or verb, i.e. any content word, and concentrate on getting the 'th' right. They shouldn't worry about 'th' in words like 'the', 'this', 'that', 'there', etc. When the students begin to improve on content words (which will usually be stressed and crucial for meaning) they can extend their concentration to 'then, this, that, these and those' (which are also usually in stressed position), and finally to 'the'. The reason for this order of priorities is that a learner will be perfectly intelligible if 'the' is always 'ze' or 'de', but if he or she says 'It's very sick' for 'It's very thick' there will be communication breakdown.

Difficulties with diphthongs

If learners have difficulty with making diphthongs draw their attention to the movement involved in terms of 'start' and 'finish' positions:

— for /ei/ as in 'm*ay*'
Start with a slightly lowered jaw. Close the jaw quite quickly, as if you were biting into a bar of chocolate.

— for /ou/ as in 's*o*'
Emphasize that the start position is relaxed, the rounding of the lips starts gradually . . . the action can be compared to the mouth movements of a fish.

— for /ai/ as in '*I*'
In the start position the lips are fairly wide apart – as for the word 'ah'. In the finish position the lips are slightly spread as for a smile. Use the comparison of biting into a slightly thicker bar of chocolate than for /ei/.

— for /ɔi/ as in 'b*oy*'
The start position has lips in an egg-shaped position; the finish position is a slight smile.

— for /au/ as in 'n*ow*'
The start position should have lips open and very slightly spread; the finish position has lips pursed (i.e. the position for whistling).

4.3.4
Vowel reduction

It is vital that learners realize the link between the placement of stress in words and vowel quality – that the vowel in the stressed syllable of a word will be a full vowel and that the vowels in unstressed syllables will be reduced to schwa. Stress placement determines vowel quality. Learners must get used to manipulating stress placement and using vowel reduction *together*. Here is an activity which is designed to establish and reinforce this aspect of spoken English.[8]

Nonsense words exercise

The exercise uses nonsense words of three syllables with the same vowel sound in each syllable. Three possible stress patterns are provided. The learner must place the stress on the syllable indicated by the stress pattern, give full vowel quality to the stressed vowel, and reduce the other vowels to schwa. As the learners work through the exercise, the teacher must carefully monitor their pronunciation. A simple form of transcription can be used – capital letters or underlining of the vowel letter to show the full vowel value, and the symbol for schwa (/ə/) written over the unstressed vowels. After each set of nonsense words with a particular vowel has been worked on, a real English word with that vowel can be given.

The student's worksheet will look something like the example on the next page.

4.3.5
Consonant clusters and sequences

We have been concentrating on the production of individual sounds, but combinations of sounds can present difficulties as well. In every language there are restrictions on groups of consonants that occur at the beginning of a word, 'initial clusters', and those that can occur at the end of a word, 'final clusters'. The restrictions are of two types: (1) restrictions on number; (2) restrictions on which consonants can co-occur and in what order. For example, in English there are initial clusters of two or three, and no more (*place*/*spl*it). In clusters of three 's' is always the first, so '*pls*it' is not a

21

Instructions: Place the stress on each of the syllables in the following nonsense words as shown by the patterns A, B, C. Pronounce the words. Be careful to use schwa in the unstressed syllables. The first two have been done for you.

	A O o o	B o O o	C o o O
(/ɑ/ as in 'fɑr')			
lalaka	lAlăkă	lălAkă	lălăkA
tapaka	tApăkă	tăpAkă	tăpăkA .
malala			
(/ɛ/ as in 'pɛt')			
chepetet			
lemepek			
senewet			
etc.			

Sample worksheet for the nonsense words exercise

possible English word. Some languages have a restriction in number of 'one', i.e. no clusters are permitted either in initial or final position or both.

If the learner's native language has, say, two as its upper limit on initial consonant clusters, then pronouncing English three-term clusters may cause problems. And even if the learner's language does have three-term initial clusters, if the learner is not used to producing particular consonants in a particular order, this may lead to problems. For example, the cluster 'spw-' may occur in the native language, but not 'spl-', so that even if /s/, /p/, and /l/ are familiar sounds, words like 'split' may be difficult to pronounce. The difficulties may be compounded if an unfamiliar sound is a member of the cluster. There may be difficulties in perception as well as production. The learner may not even hear that there are, say, three consonants at the end of a word, especially if the native language has a restriction of one or two.

There are also sequences of consonants. These may occur at word boundaries (for example, in 'last three' we have a sequence of four) or within a word (for example, in 'impossible' we have a sequence of two). We must make this distinction because the restrictions are different. Whereas English can have a sequence of 'mp' and a final cluster of 'mp' ('lamp') it does not permit an initial cluster of 'mp'.

Teaching points

If a learner has difficulty producing a particular cluster, and uses one of the coping strategies described in Chapter 2 section 2, then it may help to exploit the consonant sequences that occur in English or in the native language. For example, if the learner cannot produce the three-term final cluster in 'against', then an identical sequence could be found, such as 'one stop'. By practising the sequence, the production of the cluster may be facilitated.

It may also help if the teacher points out that new word boundaries are often created in normal connected speech. In saying the phrase 'it checked out' the final /t/ can be attached to the word 'out', so the result is something like 'it check tout'. This may help learners who use a deletion strategy and produce 'it check out'.

If the difficulties are perceptual, then the exercises described in section 3.6 should help.

**4.4
Aspects of connected speech**

An approach that involves learners in a great deal of listening, both to pre-recorded texts and to recordings of themselves, is an effective way to extend and consolidate work done on linkage and features of connected speech. Learners can be set tasks for analytical listening and self-critical listening. In doing analytical listening activities, learners discover what native speakers of English do; in self-critical listening, the learners check their own performance against a native-speaker model and their own pronunciation goals and priorities.

It is important that self-critical listening activities be limited and controlled. Learners cannot be expected to listen for several aspects of linkage and connected speech at one time. Nor should tasks be set without reference to a pre-established set of priorities. Learners should also be given some scope for choice in what they work on, even if this is limited to the teacher simply saying: 'You need to work on X, Y, and Z. Choose which of these you want to focus on in this activity.'

Because priorities may be determined by the learner's mother tongue, it may be appropriate for these activities to be done in language groups. Shared or common problems can be worked on with the whole class. (At the end of this section there are some lists for teacher reference: Rules for Linkage, Common Simplifications, and Weak Forms.)

**4.4.1
Analytical listening activities**

(Some of these activities are similar to those discussed in 3.6.)

How many words do you hear?

This activity involves presenting a phrase to the learners and asking them to indicate the word divisions, i.e. to say how many words they hear. So, for example, the teacher says or plays from a tape the natural version of 'I don't know' in which the word 'I' is pronounced very much like the article 'a' and the *t* of 'don*t*' is changed. There will be no pauses to signal the word boundaries. They listen to the phrase once or twice and say how many words they think they hear. If the learners have any difficulty, the teacher can give a slightly more explicit or full version, or help by telling them what the first word is.

After each phrase is identified, the teacher can contrast the 'full' pronunciation with the 'natural' one, and give some indication of what is happening to the sounds. In the example above, the teacher could point out the 'disappearance' of *t*.

Mini-dictation

As well as counting the words, learners can be asked to write down in normal spelling what they heard. The same strategies can be used to help – giving a slightly fuller version, or providing one of the words. The written answers can be marked to indicate aspects of pronunciation. For 'I don't know' the *t* can be crossed out, or a minus mark written over the word 'I' to show that it is 'less' than a full vowel.

Repeat exactly what you hear

Another possibility is to ask the learners to imitate as precisely as they can what they hear. The imitations can be assessed by the teacher and other class members for accuracy and this can lead to work on perception (did they hear accurately?) and production (were they able to mimic what they heard?). The teacher may also ask learners to provide a full version of what they heard. If they can do this, then the teacher can point out that the 'full' version may actually be more difficult to pronounce than the 'natural' version in some instances, and this may persuade learners of the advantages of trying to incorporate simplifications and linkages into their English.

By using a combination of analytical and self-critical listening activities, the teacher can help accustom learners to colloquial English so that they become more adept listeners, and encourage them to incorporate English-like 'blurrings' into their speech. Such activities may help learners to break down any misconceptions or misperceptions they may have about speech being a sequence of perfectly produced sounds.

4.4.2
Working on weak
forms and rhythm

As far as production skills versus perception skills are concerned, learners must be able to cope with linkage, deletions, the 'blurrings' at the edges of words, etc., that they will hear in the speech of native speakers. But they do not need to use *all* these features in their own speech. The way they themselves use linkage, for example, depends on whether they want to approximate a native accent, or not. If the former is the goal, then the learner may want to introduce 'linking r' into his or her speech; if it is not, 'linking r' is not an essential feature (see Rules for Linkage at the end of this section). Deletion or elision is another example. Learners may want to delete /t/ in phrases like 'I mus*t* be going' or 'It mus*t* be there' because they find this easier; but the use of extremely simplified forms such as 'p'raps' for 'perhaps' may actually interfere with intelligibility, and may sound strange, even 'false' or 'affected', when used by a non-native speaker. So, although learners need to be able to cope with the simplifications of English as listeners, they do not need to be able to produce all the features.

This is not so with weak forms. Not only should learners be able to cope with the weak forms they hear, they must use them when speaking English. If they do not, their speech will present listeners with a surfeit of full vowels (which will make word recognition difficult) and with a surplus of stressed forms (which may make it very difficult for the listener to find his or her way through the message and identify points of focus). There should therefore be a deliberate two-pronged approach to weak forms and the way these interact with the rhythm of English.

Unnatural speech

One interesting way of working on weak forms, rhythm, and speech simplifications is through activities built around 'unnatural speech'. Basically these activities are designed so that learners hear English sentences spoken in a very unnatural way and then, in small discussion groups, decide how the pronunciation of the sentences needs to be changed to make more natural-sounding sentences. There are two ways to obtain 'unnatural speech': one is to use a computer-linked speech synthesizer, the other is to ask someone to read a sentence as if it was just a list of words.

Let's look at the second method first. You need tape recording facilities, a reader, and a set of sentences for recording. If you simply ask the person to read aloud the sentences you will get natural formal speech. If you ask the reader to read the sentences as a list of words, the result will still probably be natural-sounding speech, because it is extremely difficult for speakers not to use normal rhythm and weak forms, and not to impose an appropriate intonation pattern onto a sentence. Even if you give someone a nonsense sentence such as, 'Apples fly quietly through the binoculars', they will still use the grammatical cues to allocate stress. The best technique is to hide the existence of sentences from the reader. This can be done by using words on flash cards, giving a list of words and revealing only one at a time, or flashing words quickly on a screen. No clues should be given about the end of the list or the reader will probably drop the pitch of the voice on the last item. One way to avoid this is to hide the sentence in a longer list. So, if you want a recording of 'He lost it' then it can be embedded in the following list 'She/he/lost/it/when/to/'.

Speech synthesis

Sentences can be synthesized by computer using any of the available speech synthesis packages.[9] Each of these packages gives sets of symbols for each sound which are used to 'feed in' the speech. The 'unnatural' words-strung-together sentences, whether they are synthesized by a computer, or concocted by reading aloud lists of words, will have a very un-English rhythm. If a speech synthesizer has been used then each syllable will be produced with the same volume, length of vowel, and clarity, as every other syllable. If the speech has been synthesized by just feeding in the sounds of the words in the sentence, then there will also be no pitch change either. If the sentences have been created by a reader, then each word will have a full explicit pronunciation – words such as 'and', 'was', 'can', 'the', etc., which usually are pronounced weakly, will have their strong pronunciation.

The task that can be set for the learners is to decide how the pronunciation of the words in the sentences must be changed to produce more natural-sounding English sentences.

Procedure

Divide the learners into pairs or small groups. Each group has a tape recording of a few sentences. For each of the sentences a context is provided. This can take several forms: it may be a brief description of the conversation the sentence came from, the actual transcript of the conversation in which the sentence occurred, or the question to which the sentence was a response. Using this information, the learners have to decide what modifications are needed. They can be guided in this task by considering the following points:

Which words should be stressed?
Which words should have their weak form?
Are there any words which have a linked or contracted form?
('don't', 'it's', 'I', 'all of', etc.)

After they have discussed the possibilities, the groups may: (1) mark a written version to show the points they would change, or (2) record the sentence themselves using a more natural pronunciation. The groups can then compare their versions, or there can be a general class discussion of the reasons for the decisions the groups have made.

In doing such exercises the teacher may want to draw the learners' attention to the 'isochronous' nature of the rhythm of English, i.e. the fact that stressed syllables occur at (roughly) regular intervals. The teacher can do this by clapping, tapping, or conducting the strong, regular beats and making sure the learners hear that a steady, rather than syncopated, rhythm is the result. This can be contrasted with the un-English rhythm of the synthesized or tape-recorded sentences which will be very even. A good way to illustrate the fact that the unstressed syllables of an English sentence are squeezed to allow the stressed syllables to fall on a regular beat is to synthesize or record 'counting' sentences such as the following:

One two three
One and a two and a three
Twenty-one, twenty-two, twenty-three

These will sound metronomic, and the teacher can contrast them with the natural '<u>One</u> an – uh <u>two</u> an – uh <u>three</u>', etc.

Re-synthesis

If microcomputer facilities are available then the students can re-synthesize the sentences incorporating changes to make the speech sound more natural. There are several simple changes that can be made that will give the desired effect. Let's say that the following sentence has been synthesized:

I would like an apple. (*Context*: What fruit would you like?)

using these symbols:

AY WHUHD LAYK AEN AEPIL[10]

The following changes can be made:

1 Insert the vowel /ə/ into each weak form, in this case, the word 'an'.

2 Insert any appropriate contracted weak forms – 'I would' becomes 'I'd'.

3 For those words which should receive stress, insert a double vowel, so 'apple' should be reprogrammed as 'AEAEPIL'

4 Programme some pitch change into the sentence.

Some speech synthesis programmes have the capability to do 4. For example, the BBC microcomputer is compatible with the 'Computer Concepts' speech synthesis programme. In this package it is possible to add variation in pitch to any vowel sound. This is done by inserting the symbol

* before the vowel that one wants to hear as stressed or prominent. (The handbook uses the word 'emphasis'.) What this symbol does is to give the vowel a slight rising then falling pitch, which will be heard as stress. So the insertion of * before the 'a' of 'apple' will give the sentence a more natural variation in pitch. It is quite clear from recent work with computer-assisted language learning that computers in the classroom have a great deal of potential, and especially that students find them very attractive, often addictive. Students who otherwise would not respond to pronunciation work may be intrigued and fascinated by speech synthesis. They may even want to try to synthesize bits of their own languages. (If they try to do this using a package designed for English, they will soon discover which of the sounds of English are not suitable for their own language, yet another way to make them aware of English pronunciation!)

Whether the activities outlined above are based on computer-synthesized speech, or on sentences created by 'list-reading', they are excellent ways to make learners realize that pronunciation is much more than pronouncing individual words correctly one after another.

Rules for linkage

Rule 1

When a word *ending* in a consonant sound is followed by a word *beginning* in a vowel sound, there is a smooth transition from one to the other. For example, in the phrase 'The dish is pretty', 'dish is' sounds exactly like 'dishes'.

Rule 2

When a word ending in a vowel sound is followed by a word beginning in a vowel sound, a transition sound which resembles either a /w/ as in 'win' or a /j/ as in 'yes' is inserted between the two vowels, according to the following rules:

(a) /w/ is added if the vowel at the end of the first word has a rounded lip position, i.e.

/u/ ('do')   /ou/ ('so')
/ɔ/ ('saw')   /au/ ('now')

Example: Please do it.

(b) /j/ is added if the vowel at the end of the word has lip-spreading (the corners of the mouth are pulled slightly back) i.e.

/ai/ ('I')   /ei/ ('say')
/i/ ('we')   /ɔi/ ('boy')

Example: We are leaving.

Rule 3

Linking r. Those British speakers who don't pronounce final 'r' will reintroduce it when the next word begins with a vowel.

Examples: more time/more interest   four pieces/four inches

25

Common simplifications of sounds (sound deletions and sound mergers)

(The list below is organized according to which sound is affected.)

1

/h/

/h/ is often deleted.

Examples: let's *h*ave   you shouldn't *h*ave   tell *h*im

2

/t/ or /d/

(a) These are often deleted when they occur between two other consonants.

Examples: firs*t* three   mus*t* be   nothing stan*d*s still   you an*d* me the fac*t* that   you mus*t* come

(b) These are often not pronounced very clearly when followed by /p/ or /b/. They are often replaced by a glottal stop, or merge into the /p/ or /b/.

Examples: a bi*t* better   ha*d* better   tha*t* picture   coul*d* be true tha*t* boy   goo*d* boy

3

/n/

(a) /n/ is pronounced more like an /m/ before /b/ or /p/.

Examples: te*n* pounds   o*n*e piece   ma*n*power

(b) /n/ is pronounced like /ŋ/ ('si*ng*') before /k/.

Examples: i*n* case   I ca*n* go   mai*n* cause

4

/s/

(a) /s/ is pronounced more like /ʃ/ as in 'shoe' before /j/ or /ʃ/.

Examples: thi*s* year   thi*s* share   thi*s* shop

5

/l/

There are some highly frequent words in which /l/ is often deleted:

Examples: a*l*ready   a*l*so   a*l*right

6

A syllable containing the unstressed /ə/ vowel is often lost:

Examples:
int(e)rest   diff(e)rent   sim(i)lar   p(e)rhaps   libr(a)ry   secret(a)ry

📼26　　　　　## List of weak forms (according to grammatical category)

		Full form	Weak form	Example*
Conjunctions	but	bʌt	bət	I want to come but I can't.
	than	ðan	ðən	He's older than she is.
	and	and	ənd/ən	He's rich and famous.
Indefinite Adjectives	such	sʌtʃ	sətʃ	Problems such as . . .
	some	sʌm	səm	There are some copies there.
	any	ɛni	əni	There aren't any more.
Personal Pronouns	he	hi	i	Does he want any?
	her	hə(r)	hə/ə(r)	I've met her mother.
	him	hɪm	ɪm	Tell him I'd like to.
	them	ðɛm	ðəm	I haven't seen them yet.
	you	ju	jə	What do you think?
	your	jɔ(r)	jə(r)	Take your time.
	us	ʌs	əs	Let us think it over.
	that	ðat	ðət	This is the house that Jack built.
Prepositions	at	at	ət	At least one.
	for	fɔ(r)	fə(r)	It's for you.
	from	frɒm	frəm	He comes from Scotland.
	of	ɒv	əv/ə	I'd love a cup of tea.
	to	tu	tə	You ought to go.
Articles	a	ei	ə	A hundred and one.
	an	an	ən	I'd like an apple.
	the	ði	ðə	That's the one.
Verbs	am	am	m	I'm going now.
	are	ɑ(r)	ə(r)	Where are you going?
	is	iz	s or z	He's here.
	was	wɒs	wəz	Was he there?
	were	wə(r)	wə(r)	We were very pleased.
	have	hav	həv/əv	They've left.
	had	had	həd or d	They had better hurry.
	has	has	əz or s	What has he done?
	do	du	dʊ/də	Do you think so?
	does	dʌz	dəz	When does he leave?
	can	kan	kən/kn	Can you hear me?
	could	kʊd	kəd	Could you do it now?
	should	ʃʊd	ʃəd	How should I know?

*Note: Both 'r-less' and 'r-pronouncing' forms are given on the tape when appropriate.

4.5
Intonation

In Chapter 3 we looked at some activities which could be used to focus learners' attention on intonation. Two points were emphasized:

— learners can 'feed on' their use of intonation in their native languages because there are many similarities across languages

— intonation is not a set of exact, complex alternatives which must be mimicked perfectly – we aren't dealing with the equivalent of tunes in a piece of music where one false note changes the melody.

In this section we will deal with these points in more detail, and discuss what the alternative approaches to teaching intonation are.

4.5.1
Alternative approaches

Benign neglect

There are various choices the teacher can make in the area of intonation. One is to ignore it completely, not using any of the awareness activities mentioned in 3.5, but leaving learners to their own intonational devices. We know that a dominant learning strategy is 'transfer from the native language' so learners will tend to use intonation in English in the ways it is used in their native language. But will this be good or bad? Will the transfer be negative or positive? Let's look at the findings of some studies which have been done comparing the use of intonation in different languages.

One such study looked at the use of rising and falling patterns.[11] It was found that for declarative sentences, thirty-five languages (including English) were reported as using a fall, but only two were reported as using a rising pattern. For question-word questions (commonly called WH-questions in English), fourteen languages (including English) were reported as using a fall and three as using a rise. For polar questions (answerable by yes or no), thirty-seven were reported as using a rise, against four using a fall. (Note that the criterion used is the link between a sentence type and an intonation pattern.) There were also similarities in the way various attitudes were conveyed through intonation. For example, Japanese question-word questions were reported as having a falling pitch, but a rise was used to convey 'extra curiosity or cordiality'; similar statements have been made about English. In French, a rising pattern on statements was used to show uncertainty; Japanese and English are said to do this as well. Since there seem to be 'intonation universals', teachers can assume fairly safely that in many cases learners will use intonation in English appropriately. So, although we know that there are differences, these universal uses indicate a way forward, that is, to use what the learner does *as the starting point* for work on intonation. Devise ways to find out what learners seem to be doing, and then reinforce the appropriate uses and modify the inappropriate ones. This approach also suggests that the starting point for teachers of monolingual classes could be the intonation of the native language. This is of course only feasible if information on the uses of intonation in the native language is available, and if the teacher and learners want to take such an analytic and comparative approach.

One final point. Many of the comparative studies that have been carried out have focused on the attitudinal uses of intonation, and on links between sentence type or function and certain intonation patterns. But this is not the 'whole story' by any means. Intonation has many different functions. We will be looking at these in 4.5.2.

Presenting 'rules'

Another alternative, one that has dominated intonation teaching, is the presentation of the patterns of English intonation in the form of rules. So the teacher becomes involved in making statements such as:

In order to do X, use pattern/tune Y.

In using this approach it is vital to remember that intonation has much in common with gesture, indeed it has been called 'vocal gesture'.[12] When we observe how people use gesture and facial expression, there seems to be a great deal of evidence that one specific gesture has a specific meaning – a smile means happiness, a frown sadness or displeasure, a wrinkled brow puzzlement. We begin to feel confident about these meaning links and claim to be able to look at someone and describe their emotional state. Much of the time we are right. But just as we begin to feel secure we are tripped up, we realize that the wrinkled brow was a sign of extreme anxiety, that the frown was simply 'concentration', and so on. We also realize that certain gestures are tied to a particular culture – the outstretched hand was not a sign of welcome, but a signal of surrender. The times when we misread a gesture remind us that gesture is relative, and sometimes idiosyncratic. The same applies to vocal gesture – intonation. Because of this, presenting rules can be dangerous. Let's look at an example.

27

In many descriptions of English intonation the fall-rise pattern is linked with 'making reservations'. Examples such as the following are given: (a) *I like his wife.* contrasted with (b) *I like his wife.* In saying (a) the speaker is said to be making a left-handed compliment. *He* is disliked, but the speaker doesn't want to say this, so opts instead for the one positive thing that can be said, holding the negative back. This is usually illustrated by giving possible continuations for (a) such as . . . *but I can't stand him/ but his family drive me mad.* But if we examine this link more carefully we see that nothing negative need be implied. There is simply something *further* to say (something has been reserved) and it may be positive or negative. So, another possible continuation is . . . *and I'm sure I'll like his parents, too.* It may very well be that our human liking for gossip brings the uncomplimentary interpretation to mind first; but the rising pattern simply has the basic meaning 'incomplete'. If a left-handed compliment is intended, then other features of communication will be present and interact with the intonation pattern, a knowing look or a grimace, for example.

It is of paramount importance that if the teacher chooses to present rules about the 'meanings of intonation' this is done in a way that makes it clear to learners that these are *tendencies*, and that encourages learners to explore and experiment with these tendencies. If we give rules that are too complex, too specific, or even too abstract, then we will probably end up stifling interest in intonation rather than encouraging it.

Teaching 'wholes' or teaching 'parts'

Many teaching materials have presented different tunes to learners and treated these as indivisible 'wholes' – the meaning of the pattern is discussed and its production is practised in drills and exercises. For example, it has been claimed that there is a specific 'contradiction' pattern in English[13] which looks something like this:

It starts with the speaker's voice very high, then the pitch drops quite sharply, then towards the end of the tune it rises slightly again. It is claimed that without having any idea of what words the speaker has said, listeners know when they hear this tune that someone is contradicting someone else. Learners are given examples of this tune such as the one below:

28

(*A and B are leaving a party*)

A: Do you want a lift?

B: You don't have a car.

Perception practice is done (contrasting the pattern with ⌒ for example), drills and exercises follow, all with the aim of inculcating the rule 'If you want to contradict someone, use this pattern.'

But there is another way of looking at this pattern. First of all, why the high starting pitch? Because the speaker is obviously 'involved' or 'interested'. B may be puzzled by A's remark (B knows that A smashed up his car last week or has been banned from driving), or completely surprised ('Has he bought another car already?'). Why the sudden drop to a lower pitch for 'have a car'? Because as far as B is concerned this is 'old or shared information or assumptions' on both their parts. You don't offer someone a lift if you don't have a car – calling a taxi or walking someone home doesn't count as a lift. Why the slight rise at the end? This probably shows that B expects some continuation. The subject is not closed. B expects a denial, some more information or an explanation. So we have three 'parts':

High start . . . low slightly rising finish . . . with very low pitch in between. Connect them up and we get:

What are the implications for this latter approach? Firstly, the learners will be dealing with a small set of 'basics' instead of a set of complex patterns or tunes. Secondly, it is a very productive approach because from these basics the learners can build up a variety of patterns. Thirdly, it's very easy to account for and explore the other possible intonations which could be used in the same situation. For example, B might have said:

1 You don't have a car.

or

2 You don't have a car.

If B chose to say 1, then he decided to treat the whole clause as 'old information' – to state the obvious ('You know that I know that you don't have a car') and to see how A responds. If B decides to say 2, then this shows he thinks that the issue which must be sorted out is the verb 'to have', so all the intonational 'umpf' is placed on that word and we get a jump up from normal starting pitch to that word and a fall from it.

If we take this approach, then we have a way to explore and analyse English intonation that takes account of the fact that speakers have choices. They use intonation to show how they perceive a particular situation and to send messages about this to listeners.

In the next section we will suggest what some of the intonation basics might be and then, in 4.5.3, suggest activities to develop the learner's control and active use of these.

4.5.2 What does intonation do?

In this section we will look briefly at the uses of intonation in English. This list of functions can form the basis of an intonation syllabus which teachers can refer to in their work on this complex aspect of pronunciation.

1 Foregrounding. *Intonation is used to put certain words in the foreground.* Speakers use pitch, along with volume, extra length on the vowel, 'full' pronunciation of consonants, etc. to give words prominence or stress. There are basically two ways in which pitch is used: (1) the speaker can make a word much higher in pitch than others, by 'jumping up' in pitch; (2) the speaker can use varying pitch, rising or falling sharply or 'wavering' in pitch to make a word stand out. (In our approach, this foregrounding function has been covered in the sections on sentence stress, but it must be remembered that pitch change is involved.)[14]

2 Backgrounding. Just as high pitch or drastically changing pitch is used to show prominence, *low pitch is used to put things in the background*, to treat something as old or shared information (as in the 'You don't have a car' example).

('Low pitch' means in the lower region of the speaker's voice range, falling or rising slightly).[15]

3 *Intonation is used to signal ends and beginnings.* For example, when a speaker is listing things, it's easy to tell when the last item has been reached because the voice pitch usually drops. Conversely, if the speaker is giving an open-ended list, the voice will not drop, but hover on a middle pitch or even rise slightly. In conversation, most people have a normal 'starting pitch'. They also have a 'finishing off' pitch, at a fairly low point in their range. Being able to tell whether a person has finished

what they are saying or not is vital in conversation. If you start speaking when your conversational partner's voice is still 'up', then this will be counted as an interruption.

4 *Intonation is used to show whether a situation is basically 'open' or 'closed'.* It may be unresolved, or incomplete, or 'open for negotiation' or confirmation, in which case a high or rising pitch is usually used. Hence the rise on open-ended lists (see above), on the conversational OK? people often use, and on statements in which something is reserved or kept back, either positive or negative, for example: 'I like his wife, (but not him).' 'Closed' situations are usually indicated by falling pitch, hence the use of falling pitch for answers to questions, strongly affirmative statements (I did do it), and some types of commands – especially where the listener is expected to comply unquestioningly: 'Do it now!'

5 *Intonation is used to show involvement.* This involvement may be emotionally highly charged, as when a speaker's voice jumps up in pitch because of anger or excitement, or it may be interest or commitment: 'You've got my attention.' It is usually possible to tell how involved someone is in a conversation by listening to the noises they make as they listen. If the listener says 'yes . . . yes . . . ah . . .' with very low pitch, this may indicate anything from utter boredom to moderate contentedness ('I'm happy to listen to you'). Noises made on quite high or even high rising pitch usually show more involvement.

6 *Intonation is used to show expectations.* The best example of this is the use of tag questions. If we say: 'He doesn't know, does he?' with a falling pitch on the tag, this shows we *expect* the answer to be: 'No, he doesn't', i.e. confirmation or agreement. We are showing through use of our voice that we have some information that we are quite sure is correct, and that we expect that the other person has that information too – it's almost a way of making what two people know explicit ('You know that I know that you know . . .'). Generally, strong expectations are shown by low falling pitch, lack of any expectations are shown by high or rising pitch. (This function is very close to 4 above.)

7 *Intonation is used to show that one speaker respects or cares about the other* (especially as regards his or her status or feelings). Such feelings can be shown in two ways:
(a) Through the use of very conventional politeness patterns. These usually consist of a higher than usual starting pitch (see 3 above) and/or a final rising pitch. A classic example is the pattern English people use when accosting someone, or as a prelude to a request ('Excuse me'.)
(b) Through the use of 'mitigation' pitch patterns. Mitigation is an attempt to soften the blow. If you are put in a position where you are forced to challenge or affront the other person (for example by having to disagree or give what you know is the *un*expected answer to a question) you show through your voice that you are unwilling or unhappy about doing this, and through this your respect for the

other person. The verbal equivalent is the frequent use of: 'Yes, but . . .' by English people in discussions or arguments. The intonation used is often a fall, and then a rise. The speaker often starts quite high in pitch as well.

8 *Intonation is used to show the relationship between the parts of a speaker's message.* Are things essentially the same, or different? In other words, speakers can show whether one point follows automatically from another, or whether it is a new dimension, or perhaps a summary of what has gone before, i.e. 'the same'. Here's an example:-

(The speaker is describing a recent argument.)
'It was just silly, really embarrassing – a total mess'.

'Just silly' gives one point of information (and will be said with falling intonation), 'really embarrassing' gives another point (so falling intonation again), but 'a total mess' may be said on a much lower pitch, because it is viewed by the speaker as a kind of summary. Or 'a total mess' could be seen as the third dimension, in which case its intonation pattern will be similar to that of the previous two points.

4.5.3
Activities

Check your facts

This activity will involve students in using 6 and 7(b) above.

Procedure
One half of the class is asked to write down five true and five false statements about themselves on slips of paper. These instructions are given in such a way that the other half of the class does not know that the students have been asked to write untruths as well as truths. The teacher collects the slips in and for each student mixes up the truths with the untruths (alternatively, the teacher can devise the untruths). The slips are handed out to the other half of the class who must interview the writers of the slips to check the accuracy of their statements. They should assume their information is accurate and should use either falling tag questions, or statements with falling intonation (for example, 'You have two older brothers', or 'You've been in England two months, haven't you?'). When the interviewer hits upon an untruth, the interviewee must set him or her right, but in a very polite way. Telling the students that the interview is an official one – a job interview perhaps – is one way to make clear the need for mitigation. Useful phrases such as 'Not really . . .'; 'I wouldn't say that was the case . . .'; 'Actually, no . . .'; 'Well no . . .', can be provided. The teacher circulates and monitors the appropriate use of intonation.

The interrupting game[16]

This activity requires the use of intonation to mark ends and beginnings (see use 3).

Procedure
The teacher (or a volunteer student) starts to talk on any topic. Anyone in the class can interrupt him or her, using one of the following openers:

'Excuse me for interrupting . . .'; 'I'd like to say something here . . .'; 'May I ask a question . . .', etc. The speaker must respond and then get back to the topic. The following phrases can be provided:

Anyway   In any case   As I was saying   Where was I?
To go on with my story

The class members can be told their job is to sidetrack the speaker; the speaker can be told to try to finish the narrative as coherently as possible despite all the interruptions. When the speaker gets back to the topic, generally low pitch should be used to show continuation. The interrupters must listen carefully for the best times to interrupt – everyone shouldn't yell out at once.

First impressions[17]

This activity relates to use 4, and exploits the fact that people often feel they can tell a lot about a person from their appearance.

Procedure
The teacher provides photographs of people. These must be people the teacher knows or knows about (not anonymous pictures in a magazine). In pairs, class members ask each other questions such as: 'What's his/her age?' (job, nationality); 'Is s/he happy?' (content, trustworthy); 'Would you like him or her as a friend?', etc. Strong impressions should be delivered with low, falling intonation, more speculative ones with rising intonation or perhaps a high pitched opener ('Well . . . uh . . . mmm'). The class tries to formulate a composite image of the person and discusses its reasons for particular judgements. The true information is then revealed.

A possible variant is to provide photographs of actors 'in character'. At the end of the discussion the class can be told about the character the actor was portraying and decide if their face/expression/demeanour had succeeded in conveying the essentials of the character.

The 'Perfect Gift'

This activity encourages learners to use intonation to show interest/involvement (see use 5).

Procedure
Students interview each other in pairs about their likes/dislikes, interests, etc. Another pair is assigned to listen in and their task is to find out what each person likes best so they can think up a 'perfect gift' for each. The activity should be billed as a cooperative one and the speaking pair should try to reveal as much as possible about themselves. They may give very strong hints, but they must not say directly, 'I've always wanted a _____.' The listening pair must try to detect from the intonation what each person is most enthusiastic about. They should discuss this between themselves and decide on the 'perfect gift' for each. The listeners then reveal their decisions and the receivers reveal their satisfaction or dissatisfaction.

'Sets and Subsets'

This is a simple activity which can be used to check on the learners' ability to give 'closed' and 'open' lists (see uses 3/4).

Procedure

Learners work in pairs, separated by a screen. One learner has assembled on his/her table sets of similar objects (or picture cards), for example, pieces of fruit, items of jewellery, cosmetics, crockery, etc. The teacher comes around and makes subsets of each set of items – sometimes the subset can actually be the complete set. The learner looking at the items names them; the partner must decide whether: (1) all the items of a particular type have been named; or (2) there are more items from the same set left on the table. He or she signals this by saying 'full set' for (1) and 'subset' for (2) . The lister's voice should convey this information; a rising intonation on the last item shows there are other items left, a falling intonation shows the subset is actually the full set. So for example, if there is a plate, a cup, a saucer, a mug, and a soup bowl as items of crockery, and the teacher forms a subset of cup, mug, and saucer, the lister should keep the voice high on the third item of the list. After each list the pair check on their success and give themselves a total score at the end.

'Handle with Care'

This activity is designed to develop the use of politeness patterns and mitigation (see use 7). The teacher (or a volunteer student) makes some over-the-top statement on an issue (for example, 'Smoking should be banned'; 'There should be no age restriction on drinking'). The class members must respond without making any direct statements of disagreement, but politely and diplomatically. Phrases such as: 'Do you really think that?'; 'Surely you don't mean that?'; 'That's an extreme view don't you think?' can be provided. The need to be polite and gentle can be justified by asking students to imagine that the speaker is older/ respected/ has 'high' status and that they are younger/subordinates, etc. (The role play activity 'Spokesman and Aide' described in 4.2.1 can be used in a similar way.)

'Alibi'

The teacher announces that a crime has been committed by at least two people at a specified time and place, for example: the railway station, Wednesday, between 6 and 8 pm. Two students take on the roles of police investigators. It is their job to find out who the prime suspects are. Most of the other class members are given alibi cards which describe their whereabouts at the time the crime was committed. Some of the alibi cards are identical – two people were together and so can corroborate each other's alibi. The remaining students are given witness cards which conflict with the other cards, for example: 'You saw Maria walking past the Post Office at 6.30 pm', when Maria's card says: 'You were in the pub with Juan between 5.30 and 9 pm'. The investigators must question each person about his or her whereabouts. The replies should be very positively stated (see use 4: 'closed' situations).

Students who can corroborate another student's alibi should do so (again with assertive, low falling intonation). Throughout the activity the teacher should monitor the use of low falling intonation for assertions, denials, claims, counter-assertions.

4.5.4
Representing pitch

When working on intonation, there are various ways that pitch can be represented. Lines can be drawn across the words to indicate direction of pitch movement: 'I saw you there'. Or words can be written on cards and moved about on a magnetic board or felt screen.

saw

I	you	there.

Arrows can also be used to give a general indication of pitch movement.

↘ I saw you there.

References

1 See Chapter 10 in P. Ladefoged *A Course in Phonetics* (Harcourt, Brace, Jovanovich 1975).
2 Adapted from a suggestion from teachers at Davies's Eurocentre, Brighton.
3 J. K. Jerome *Three Men on the Bummel* (published 1900, Penguin edition 1983).
4 For /k/ in 'cool' the tongue is further back.
5 P. McCarthy *The Teaching of Pronunciation* (Cambridge University Press 1978).
6 British people are most familiar with this sound as the substitute for medial 't' in Cockney speech.
7 From B. J. Wenk 'Articulatory Setting and De-fossilisation' (*Interlanguage Studies Bulletin* 4 1979) which suggested this technique.
8 Taken from H. B. Woods *Syllable Stress and Unstress* (Anglais Langue Seconde 1979).
9 Some widely available packages are: Computer Concepts (for BBC Micro), Gaddesdon Place, Hemel Hempstead, Herts and Orator VSM2128 (General Instrument).
10 These symbols are used by Orator (see note 9).
11 A. Cruttenden 'Falls and Rises: Meanings and Universals' (*Journal of Linguistics* 17 1981).
12 D. Bolinger 'Intonation and its Parts' (*Language* 58/3 1982).
13 M. Liberman and I. Sag 'Prosodic Form and Discourse Function' (*Chicago Linguistic Society* 10 1974).
14 This function has been termed 'tonic placement' by some analysts.
15 Compare Brazil et al, 'referring tone', in *Discourse Intonation and Language Teaching* (Longman 1980).
16 Taken from E. Keller *Gambits* (Canadian Public Service Commission, Ottawa 1976).
17 Taken from V. J. Cook *Using Intonation* (Longman 1979).

5

Sounds and spellings

Very often pronunciation teaching has focused on the important sound contrasts and has almost totally ignored the way these sounds are represented in writing and their role in the learners' pronunciation development. It has often been claimed that English spelling is totally irregular. This is not the case. We begin by looking at the way English spelling works.

**5.1
How does the
English spelling
system work?**

In the following section we will outline some basic features of the English spelling system. This will serve as a context and background for the rules which will be presented in section 5.4.

Feature 1
The first feature hardly needs stating – the English writing system is an alphabetic one. It follows the convention that there is a correspondence between letters and individual sounds. However, unlike the spelling system of some other languages which use an alphabet, several of the letters in English can have more than one sound value. So there is not always a strict one-to-one correspondence between sound and letter. Some letters do have only one value – they can be called 'single-valued' ('d', 'p' and 'm' are examples); some letters can have two or more values – they can be called 'multi-valued' (an example is 'c' which can represent the sound in 'cat' or the sound in 'city').

Feature 2
In the English spelling system, a 'root' or 'base' is always spelled the same. For example, in the pair 'sign' and 'signal' the root s-i-g-n is invariable; it is always represented with the same sequence of four letters even though in the first word the vowel 'i' has the value /ai/ as in 'mine' and the 'g' is silent, and in the second word, the vowel 'i' has the value /ɪ/ as in 'fit' and the 'g' is not silent but represents the sound /g/ as in 'go'. Each root or base has a unique spelling.

This feature makes English spelling a highly 'visual' system in the sense that the reader can very easily recognize related words. For example, when a person sees the word 'photogravure', he or she will immediately recognize the root p-h-o-t-o and know that this word is somehow related to 'photograph', 'photography', 'photographic', even though the person has never seen the word before. We can use the example given above to demonstrate the advantages of this. The word 'sign' could be more 'phonetically' spelled as 'sine' but the relatedness of these two words is not nearly so strongly indicated to the reader by the spellings 'sine' and 'signal' as it is by the spellings 'sign' and 'signal'.

We can see another example of this visual principle at work if we consider the grammatical endings in English. These are always spelled the same even though they might not be pronounced the same. The regular past tense ending is always spelled as '-ed' even though it represents different sounds in 'wanted', 'filled' and 'rushed'.

This visual principle works in another interesting way. Two words which are unrelated and different in meaning tend to be 'separated' visually for the reader by their spellings even though they may sound the same when said. 'Ruff' and 'rough' are not related in meaning at all, and they are spelled differently. Interestingly, this would seem to explain why there are very few pairs of words in English which are written the same but are pronounced differently (called *homographs*). 'Read' (verb infinitive) and 'read' (verb past tense) is an example. But there are quite a few pairs which sound the same but are written differently (called *homophones*). Some examples are 'sun' and 'son', 'won' and 'one', 'threw' and 'through', and 'would' and 'wood'. In all cases these words are unrelated in meaning and are kept apart in the spelling as well.[1] These first two features reveal something very important about the English system – it pays attention to individual sounds, and it also pays attention to larger units, i.e. 'roots' and the elements of the grammar.

Feature 3

Some of the symbols used in the writing system are combinations of two or more letters from the alphabet. One could call them 'composite' symbols. For example, '-ph-' represents the sound in /f/ as in 'fish' (examples are 'phase', 'physical', 'phone'). '-th-' can represent two sounds: the one in 'thick' or the one in 'there'. '-gh-' can represent the sound /g/ as in 'go' in a very small set of words like 'ghost' and 'ghoul' or it can have the value of 'silence' as in 'through', 'thorough', or /f/ in 'cough'.

Note that these composite symbols can therefore be single-valued or multi-valued too.

Feature 4

Some of the symbols are used to signal something about another symbol. They have no sound value themselves when they are functioning in this way. The clearest example of this is the letter 'e' at the end of a word; it tells the reader something about the value of the preceding vowel letter. This is the so-called 'silent -e'. In the word 'Pete' it signals that the preceding 'e' is pronounced as /i/ as in 'feet' (compare 'e' in 'pet'). Final 'e' is also used to signal something about a preceding consonant: in the word 'cage' it indicates that the 'g' has the value of /dʒ/ as in 'jet', not /g/ as in 'go'. In 'ice' it signals that the letter 'c' is pronounced as /s/.

Feature 5

Position and surroundings are extremely important in the English system. We've said that '-gh-' can represent the sound /f/ as in 'fish', but it can only do this at the end of a word. 'Wh-' can only occur at the beginning of words; '-ng' can only occur at the end. When position and surroundings are taken into account, some very regular patterns and sound values for letters emerge, as we shall see.

In summary, English spelling is not purely 'phonetic' although it is quite substantially phonetic. If 'regularity' is defined as a direct and invariable one-to-one correspondence between symbol and sound, then it is not completely regular. But regularity can be looked at in another way – the regular and unique representation of any of the units of a language. In that sense, English spelling is quite regular; roots and grammatical endings have invariable representations. It is important to recognize that English writing represents the language at two levels at the same time: the level of sound and the level of units of meaning. This is a complex situation and of course there will be exceptions to many of the rules. Many of these exceptions are due to the history of the language and the vast amount of borrowing that has taken place from other languages. (Although merely knowing this gives neither learners nor teachers much comfort!) Despite the complexity of the system (or should we say systems) it is a major pronunciation resource for non-native learners.

In section 5.4 we will look at the rules and regularities of the system in more detail. But first we must consider some points concerning the way learners use the writing system as readers and as writers.

5.2
English spelling and learning pronunciation

5.2.1
English spelling and readers and writers

We have to consider the way language users deal with the spelling system in two different situations – the situation of the reader and that of the writer. In writing, a person has to recall the spelling of a word that he or she wants to write down, something must be pulled out of the memory. Very occasionally the writer has to decide how to write a particular word that he or she has never before seen in print. In reading, a person uses the patterns on the page to decide how to pronounce a particular word. Of course this isn't necessary when reading silently, but if asked to read aloud, and there is, say, an unfamiliar surname in the text, the reader must use what he or she knows about the spelling conventions of the language to arrive at a possible pronunciation. The problems of the reader and the writer are not the same; the latter must recall patterns, and the former must decipher or decode patterns. In English the reader's problem is actually usually simpler than the writer's. For instance, some letters are sometimes silent in a small set of words. In 'knowledge' the 'k' is not pronounced, in 'gnostic' the 'g' is not pronounced, nor are the 'm' or 'p' in 'mnemonic' and 'pneumonia'. Note that these silent letters occur before the letter 'n'. The writer must remember that it is a 'k' that belongs before the 'n' in 'knowledge' not a 'g', that it is a 'g' that belongs before the 'n' in 'gnostic' not a 'k'; but all the reader has to remember when he or she is reading aloud and comes across one of these words is that the letter before the 'n' is silent.

5.2.2
Differences in the
way natives and
non-natives use
the system[2]

A native speaker of English most often has to grapple with the spelling system of the language as writer; words whose meaning and pronunciation are well-known have to be written down, and it is in this situation that native speakers become very conscious of the intricacies of the English spelling system. Only occasionally do we have to attempt to write an unknown word. With non-native learners of English the predominant problem is usually how to pronounce an unknown word in a written text. Of course in English class the teacher is there and can provide the pronunciation, but when the student is out in an English-using environment and 'on his own' new and unfamiliar words will be met, many of them in written texts, and learners need to be equipped with a knowledge of the spelling conventions of English in order to decide how to pronounce them. If the learner cannot function independently in this way, then passive reading vocabulary will remain passive, and the learner will not be able to put words to active oral use. Of course, dictionaries can be consulted, but all learners know that this is a time-consuming and sometimes impossible strategy. It is far more efficient to be able to predict the pronunciation of a word from the way it is spelled, even if this means coming up with two possible pronunciations which can then be 'tried out' on listeners. Because English has become an international language, learners may recognize many English words when reading and speakers of European languages in particular may be able to relate them to cognate words in their own languages, but the pronunciation may still be a problem. Learners who will be using English for academic study and those who need English to read scientific and technical texts will meet many new words. If, during their period of English classroom learning, they are taught strategies for arriving at the pronunciation of words and develop confidence in using these strategies, then their passive 'reading vocabulary' can be put to active oral use if necessary. Despite all that is claimed about the irregularity of the English spelling system, it provides a great deal of information about the pronunciation of words – if it did not, it could not properly be called an alphabetic system. Not all writing systems do this – for instance Chinese characters give virtually no information about pronunciation. (This means that a speaker of a particular dialect of Chinese can read what a speaker of a different dialect has written even though he or she could not understand the same words when spoken.)

The English spelling system is rich in both regularities and irregularities which present problems to non-native learners (and to English-speaking children learning to write their language). But, through a mixture of direct instruction and their own use of the powerful tool of inference, learners can become efficient users of the system. It is the teacher's job to present rules that are *usable* and to make sure that learners are inferring correctly. Their correct inferences should be reinforced, and praised; those which are incorrect (where the system or their own language experience has misled them) need to be changed. In the next section we will look at the way learners can be misled – at the sources of spelling-induced pronunciation problems.

5.3
The causes of spelling problems

When dealing with spelling errors, it is sometimes useful if the teacher understands the source of the error. There are several possible causes of spelling difficulties among non-native learners:

1 Among learners whose native languages use the Roman alphabet, as English does, problems may be caused by confusion between the sound value of a particular letter in the native language and its value in English. For example, in German the letter 'v' represents the sound /f/ as in 'fun'; in English it represents the sound /v/ as in 'vision'. So, a German-speaking learner may read the word 'drive' to rhyme with 'life'. The strategy learners are using could be put something like this: 'When I'm not sure what the sound/spelling correspondence is in English, I assume it is the same as that in my native language.' Very often, learners seem to resort to this strategy when they are 'under pressure', for example when they are asked to read aloud before the class or onto tape, or when the text they are dealing with contains a very large number of words which are unfamiliar to them, or (in the situation of writer) when they are doing a dictation or written test. It may be that the sound/spelling conventions of the native language do not so much interfere, as provide a quick 'escape route' when the learner is in a tight spot. In many cases, it is very likely that learners are all too aware of the 'danger', and therefore never experience any cross-spelling-system confusion, but sometimes some very odd things happen. For example, German learners of English quickly realize as soon as they meet written English forms that the letter 'w', which in German stands for /v/ as in 'very' (examples: 'wenn, weil, wollen'), has a different value in English. It corresponds to /w/ as in 'weather', 'will', and 'wet'. Now this is a new sound for the learners (it does not occur in German), so they will be very careful to pronounce words like 'will' and 'weather' correctly. The desire to avoid making a mistake may actually cause an 'over-reaction', and some learners begin to pronounce English words beginning with 'v' with the new sound /w/ as well! So 'very' and 'value' become 'wery' and 'walue'.

2 Learners whose native language uses a non-alphabetic system will have to adjust to alphabetic conventions. Japanese uses a system in which a symbol represents a syllable, not an individual sound. In Arabic script, the representation of vowels is variable – they can be represented in the writing system, but may be omitted in certain styles and types of script.

3 Another source of difficulty is the English spelling system itself. As soon as learners are exposed to written English, they start to make generalizations about how the system works. Since English is an alphabetic system, this means basically sorting out which letter corresponds to which sound. But as we have seen, English spelling is not a strictly regular alphabetic system in which one letter always stands for one sound and one sound only. Learners whose native languages do work in this way (Spanish and Italian are the two best examples) may find this more difficult to adjust to than learners who are aware that their own language's spelling is not strictly 'phonetic', as, for example,

French speakers may be. Because of some of the irregularities of English spelling, the errors that non-native learners make will very often be the same as the errors made by native speakers, especially English children who are learning to write their language. These errors are due to incorrect guesses about the nature of the system, and sometimes are aggravated by the fact that some very common, high-frequency words have exceptional spellings. For example, the rule that 'gh' at the end of a word is silent is broken by only seven words, but one of these is 'enough'.

4 Finally, there is the pronunciation of the learner. If a learner has difficulty in distinguishing English /p/ as in 'pet' from English /b/ as in 'bet', then, in doing a dictation, he or she may spell 'pill' as 'bill'. Here is another example. In a dictation given to a class, the surname 'Rogers' occurred. A Japanese learner wrote this as 'Largerse'. The misspelling of the first letter is surely due to the problem Japanese learners have in distinguishing /r/ as in 'run' from /l/ as in 'love'. The probable sources of errors for various languages are listed below.

Spelling and pronunciation errors

Note: The numbers in column three refer to the causes of problems listed above.

Error[3]	Native language	Possible cause
understand written as *underestand*	Spanish	4 Learners often insert a short vowel before -st clusters
vocabulary written as *vocavulary*	Spanish	1 Spanish has a /b/ sound which is written as 'b' or 'v' at the beginning of words and another sound which only occurs in the middle of words also written as 'b' or 'v'
language written as *lenguage*	Spanish	4 Learners often confuse /a/ and /ɛ/ (bat-bet)
resale written as *resell*	Chinese	4 When /ei/ (sale) occurs before a consonant Chinese learners tend to substitute /ɛ/ (sell)

Spelling and pronunciation errors cont.

Error	Native language	Possible cause
*Chr*istchurch pronounced as /tʃ/ in '*ch*eck' followed by /r/	Thai	3 The two letters *ch* can have the value /k/ before 'r'
impressive stress on last syllable pronounced to rhyme with 'five'	French	3 Learner overgeneralizing silent -e rule (only applies in stressed syllables)
answer 'w' pronounced instead of silent	French	3 Learner not aware of exceptional spelling
bulletin first syllable to rhyme with '*beau*ty'	Polish	3 Learner has overgeneralized value of 'u' from words like 'm*u*sic', '*u*se', etc
special pronounced '*spech-el*'	Italian	1 Italian '*ci*' has the value /tʃ/ (*ch*eck)
describe written as *descripe*	German	3 Alternation of /b/p/ in descri*b*e – descri*p*tion *or* 4 Learner pronounces final /b/ as /p/
writing written as *writting*	Arabic	3 Learner not aware of the fact that double consonants usually indicate a short vowel value
people written as *ppl*	Arabic	2 Vowels often not represented in Arabic script

5.4
Rules and regularities of English spelling

In this section we will examine some of the regularities of English spelling and suggest some ways of working on them with learners. Before learners can use the rules[4] that will be presented, they will need to be familiar with certain notions. These are:

1 The notion of *consonant* and *vowel*. Learners must be able to distinguish between consonant letters and vowel letters. It is fairly simple to say that English has five vowel letters 'a,e,i,o,u' and that the rest of

the letters (21 in all) are consonant letters. The letter 'y' is the only troublesome one; it sometimes stands for a vowel sound, as in 'by', 'city', or 'physical' and sometimes for a consonant sound, as in 'yet' or 'yellow'. (Note that it always stands for a consonant when it is at the beginning of a word, and that when it is somewhere in the middle or at the end of a word, it stands for a vowel sound.)

Learners need this information to develop a visual sensitivity to spelling patterns. For example, they must be able to say that 'cat' has the sequence consonant-vowel-consonant, or CVC for short, and that 'rest' is consonant-vowel-consonant-consonant, or CVCC.

2 Learners need to be able to identify *affixes*. There are two types: *prefixes*, which are units with a basic meaning which can be added to the beginning of a word (for example, 'un-' which has the meaning 'opposite' or 'not' as in 'unhappy', 'unusual' or 'unwise') and *suffixes*, which can be added to the end of a word (for example, '-ion', which changes a verb into a noun; or '-ist', which denotes the person who performs the action of a verb, or who is concerned with that activity).

3 Learners must be aware of the notion of *syllable* and must be able to identify how many syllables a word has.

These notions are not needed for work on the spelling system alone, they have relevance and usefulness for other aspects of the use of the English language.

As we said in section 5.2, non-native speakers have to grapple with English spelling most often as readers. Of course, they do also have to remember spellings to write, but some learners have very limited writing requirements. Therefore, the following section will concentrate on rules which learners can exploit as readers.

Rules for consonants
Sound values of single consonant letters

The following consonant letters have one sound value only.

Table 1

Letter	Sound	Letter	Sound
d	as in: do, bad	r	as in: right
f	as in: fun, half, before	v	as in: vision, live
j	as in: jet	x	as in: fix
m	as in: me, arm	y	as in: yet, yellow
n	as in: no, an, another	z	as in: zoo
p	as in: put, up	t	as in: to, put

Sound values of single consonant letters cont.

The following letters also regularly represent one sound, but for each of these there are a small number of cases where the letter has a different value.

Table 1.1

Letter	Sounds	Letter	Sounds
b	as in: bad, job	k	as in: kit
	(but 'silent' in bomb, lamb, subtle)		(but silent in knee, knowledge)
h	as in: he, ahead	l	as in: lip, crucial
	h is pronounced when it occurs at the beginning of a stressed syllable with these exceptions: honest, hour, honour, heir		(but silent in would, could, should)
		w	as in: weather, will
			(but silent in two, answer, write)

Because all the letters in Table 1.1 have a regular sound value, except in cases where they are not sounded at all (that is, are 'silent'), they can probably be included in the set in Table 1. This would mean that there are seventeen out of nineteen consonant letters that show a regular one-letter/one-sound correspondence. When learners meet the words in Table 1.1, they can be told that these are 'strange' spellings. The fact that some of the words in Table 1.1 are very common, frequently occurring words probably helps the situation.

The following single consonant letters can have two sound values.

Table 2

Letter	Sounds	Letter	Sounds
c	can be /k/ as in: cat or /s/ as in: city	g	can be /g/ as in: go or /dʒ/ as in: cage
	(also, rarely, the sound represented by 'ch' in 'church', for example 'cello')		(also sometimes the sound represented by 's' as in 'pleasure' (/ʒ/) Examples are: garage, prestige, etc., but this varies from speaker to speaker.)

Whether 'c' represents /k/ or /s/ is determined by a very simple rule. It represents /s/ when it is followed by 'i', 'e' or 'y', and /k/ everywhere else.

The same pattern applies to 'g' although there are some exceptions. 'g' has the value /dʒ/ when it is followed by 'i', 'e' or 'y' and it represents /g/ everywhere else. But as exceptions we have 'give', 'girl', 'anger', 'eager', 'get', 'gear'. There aren't very many exceptions but some of them are very common words.

When single consonant letters are doubled in English, they keep the same sound value.

Table 3

Letters	Sounds
bb	as in: ebb
dd	as in: odd
ff	as in: ruff
gg	as in: egg or for the value /dʒ/: suggest and exaggerate
ll	as in: call
nn	as in: inn

Letters	Sounds
pp	as in: stopping
rr	as in: purr
ss	as in: mass
tt	as in: putt
zz	as in: jazz
cc	as in: tobacco (but can be /ks/ in accept)

Sound values of composite consonant letters

English uses composite consonant letters. Two or three letters represent one sound. The following have only one sound value.

Table 4

Letters	Sound
ck	as in: pick
le	as in: bottle
ng	as in: sing
tch	as in: watch
wh	as in: which

Letters	Sound
ph	as in: phone, graph
sh	as in: shut, wash
qu	regularly represents the sequence of the sounds /k/ followed by /w/ as in: quick, sequence

There are also some positional restrictions which are useful to learners.

'ck', 'le', 'tch', 'ng' never occur at the beginning of words
'qu', 'wh' never occur at the end of words
'ph', 'sh' can occur at the beginning or end of words

Two composite letters have two possible sound values.

1 'ch' can represent the sound as in 'chip' (/tʃ/).
   Examples: choice, champion, change, child, chocolate
   'ch' can also represent /k/ as in 'kit'.
   Examples: character, chorus, chord, Christmas, chlorine, technical

   Note that when 'ch' occurs at the end of words, it always has the value of the sound in choice, change, child.
   Examples: each, reach, rich, peach, church

2 'gh' can represent the sound /f/ as in 'fish'.
   Examples: enough, tough, cough, toughen, coughing
   'gh' can also stand for 'silence'.
   Examples: though, through, taught, daughter
   (Note that there are about five words where 'gh' represents /g/ as in 'go'. *Examples*: ghetto, ghost, ghastly, ghoul, gherkin.)

Rules for vowels

The correspondences between vowel sounds and vowel letters are very complex, but there are some very clear patterns which can be extremely useful for the learner.

Single vowel letters in monosyllabic words

Each of the single vowel letters, 'a, e, i, o, and u' has two principal sound values.

Table 5

Letter	Sound 1	Sound 2
a	/ei/ (hate)	/a/ (hat)
e	/i/ (Pete)	/ɛ/ (pet)
i	/ai/ (mine)	/ɪ/ (fit)
o	/ou/ (note)	/ɒ/ (not)
u	/ju/ (cute)	/ʌ/ (cut)

To decide which of its two possible sounds a letter in a word stands for, we must look at what letters follow the vowel letter in the word. If we do this we find three patterns.

Pattern A
If the single vowel letter is followed by a single consonant letter, then the vowel sound will be the one in column 2. Other examples are:

hop   bat   bit   nut   kit   sit   set   bed   cat
red   sat   top

Pattern B
If the single vowel letter is followed by two consonant letters, it will also have the sound in column two. Other examples are:

rest   past   must   cost   film   cross   half   bulb
lump   knock

In some accents, notably R P, there is also the value /ɑ/ for letter 'a' in this pattern.

Pattern C
If the single vowel letter is followed by a consonant and the letter 'e' (at the end of the word) the single vowel letter will represent the sound in column 1. Other examples are:

cake   make   side   joke   mute   home   came
like   hole   June   while

This is the 'silent e' rule which English children are taught at school, usually in one of the following formulas:

'When two vowels go walking, the first one does the talking.'

or

'An 'e' at the end of a word makes the vowel say its name.' (i.e. the letter name used when reciting the alphabet.)

The values in columns 1 and 2 are often referred to as the 'long' and 'short' sounds, respectively. But these terms are really inaccurate because vowel length in English is not a constant, the vowels in column 1 are not always longer than those in column 2. If we compare the column 2 value for 'e' (which is /ɛ/ in 'bed') and the column 1 value for 'e' (which is /i/ in 'Pete'), we find that the vowel in 'bed' is held just as long as the vowel in 'Pete'. The length of a vowel in English depends on what sounds follow it in a word.

Learners should be presented with these rules, and encouraged to use them actively. Whenever words that do not conform to these rules are met (and there are exceptions of course), this should be pointed out to them.

Single vowel letters in polysyllabic words

How do native English speakers know that the single vowel letter 'a' represents /ei/ as in 'mate' in the word 'relation', but /a/ as in 'mat' in the word 'action'? Or that the vowel letter 'e' represents /i/ as in 'Pete' in 'completion', but /ɛ/ as in 'pet' in 'congestion'? Compare also 'lotion' with 'option', and 'confusion' with 'production'. In all these examples the suffix ending is the same, and therefore the stress pattern is the same – stress falls on the syllable before the suffix. The rule is quite simple; all you have to do is count the number of consonants following the vowel. The first step in operating the rule is to ignore the suffix ending, in this case '-ion'. Now look at the single vowel letter. Let's take the examples with 'a'. What follows 'a' in 'relation'? One consonant – 't'. Now what follows 'a' in 'action'? Two consonants – 'c' followed by 't'. The rule is: when a single vowel letter is followed by two consonants, it has its 'short' (column 2) value; when it is followed by one consonant, it has its 'long' (column 1) value.[5] The value of 'a' in 'relation' can be predicted if one knows that this word is actually 'relate-ion' and the 'silent e' has been deleted. The same can be said of 'completion' and 'confusion'. But what about 'lotion'? There is no word 'lote' to which the learner can be referred. For many of these words learners *can* refer to a word that ends in a silent 'e'. For some of these words there is no other form to refer to. They can then count the consonants.

This rule works for the single letters 'a', 'e', 'o' and 'u'. Here are some more examples:

nation   depletion   notion   dilution   facial   substantial
menial   dubious

It does not work for the letter 'i'; we have 'provision', where 'i' is followed by one consonant, and 'subscription' where it is followed by two consonants (again ignoring the suffix letters 'i-o-n'), but 'i' has its short value (/ɪ/) in both words.

Note that in the above set of examples, words with the suffixes '-ious' and '-ial' have been included. This rule applies to any word which has a suffix in which the letter 'i' is followed by a vowel, and then anything else. The crucial sequence is a suffix with 'i' and then a vowel. So it works for the following suffixes:

-ion -ial -ious -ian -ia -iar -io -ior -ium -ius -iate -ient
-iant -iary -iable

In other words, it works for one sub-group of the large group of suffixes which cause stress to be placed on the syllable before the suffix (see section 4.1 on word stress).

This rule is extremely useful because there are something like 10,000 words in English with these 'i-vowel' endings and the rule will predict the pronunciation of the vowel letter in the stressed syllable in 99.9 per cent of the cases. If the learners can operate this rule then they have a powerful weapon to use in their attempts to sort out the sound value of the single vowel letter in polysyllabic words.

Vowel digraphs

English has eighteen composite vowel symbols in which a sequence of two vowel letters stands for a single vowel sound. We can call these *digraphs*. In contrast to the single vowel letters, these digraphs do not change their sound value in stressed or unstressed position. Already this makes up for the fact that there are eighteen of them! For example, 'eu' in 'neutral' represents the same sound as it does in 'neutrality' even though it is in stressed position in 'neutral' and in unstressed position in 'neutrality'. Here is another example: 'au' represents the same vowel sound in both 'cause' and 'causality'. This is in striking contrast to what happens to single vowel letters. Compare the value of 'o' in 'melody' and 'melodious' (although as we have seen above the value of 'o' in 'melodious' is predictable).

The eighteen vowel digraphs actually occur less frequently than the single vowel letters and their occurrence is restricted to certain positions. For example, 'ai', 'au', 'ei', and 'eu' rarely occur at the ends of words; 'ie', 'oa' rarely occur at the beginnings of words. But, most importantly from the learner's point of view, each vowel digraph has *one* major value. (The definition of 'major' is based on frequency – in 100 words with, say, 'ui' it will stand for a particular sound in the majority of the words.) There may be a few minor values, and some of these may occur in very common, high-frequency words, but when one meets a new word with a particular vowel digraph, the chances that it represents its 'major value' are very high indeed.

The following list gives: (1) the major value of each digraph with some example words; (2) the minor value(s) with examples that are very common 'core' vocabulary items; (3) any positional restrictions. This information is designed for teacher reference, and can be useful when responding to questions from learners about spelling and pronunciation, or working out the pronunciation of a new word with the class, or considering how to deal with spelling mistakes in students' writing, It's not appropriate to present the material in this form to learners, who need to work towards an 'automatic' response.

English vowel digraphs

au/aw

Major value	Minor value
/ɔ/	/a/*
cause	laugh
claw	aunt

* or /ɑ/ depending on accent

Restrictions on position: as is clearly shown by the examples above, 'au' occurs before consonants and rarely at the end of words; 'aw' is the digraph that occurs at the end of a word. (mawt and plau look odd.)

'ea'

Major value	Minor values
/i/	/ei/
each	break
reach	steak
eat	great
meat	/ɛ/
heat	dead
Keats	head
peat	instead
bead	ready
lead (verb)	weather
read (infinitive)	
	(before -sure)
	measure
	pleasure
	(before l)
	wealth
	health

ee

Major value	Minor value
/i/	/ɪ/
bleed	been (weak form)
seed	
need	

ei/ey

Major value	Minor values
/ei/	/ai/
obey	height
reign	eye
	either
	/i/
	either
	key
	receive

Restrictions on position: 'ei' usually appears before a consonant; 'ey' appears at the end of a word.

English vowel digraphs cont.

eu/ew

Major value	*Minor value*
/ju/ or /u/	/ou/
few	sew
crew	
new	
neutral	
eulogy	

ie

Major values	*Minor value*
/ai/	/ɛ/
die	friend
tie	
lie	
pie	

/i/
achieve
believe

Restrictions on position: note that when 'ie' occurs in final position in monosyllables, it has the value /ai/; but when it occurs in the middle of a word it has the value /i/.

oa

Major value	*Minor value*
/ou/	/ɔ/
coat	broad
goat	

oi/oy

Major value	*No minor values*
/ɔi/	
boy	
toy	
joy	
coy	
coin	
join	
loin	
coil	
foil	

Restrictions on position: the examples show that 'oy' can occur at the end of words, but 'oi' cannot – it occurs before consonants. (boyt and poi look very strange.)

oo

Major value	Minor values
/u/	/ʌ/
boot	blood
root	flood
	/ʊ/
	foot
	book

ui

Major value	Minor value
/ju/ or /u/	/ɪ/
suit	biscuit
bruise	build

ou/ow

Major value	Minor values
/au/	/ʌ/
crown	couple
town	trouble
trout	enough
	/ɔ/
	cough
	/ou/
	owe
	own
	shoulder
	/u/
	group
	soup
	routine

This pair of vowel digraphs is notoriously difficult. In fact, there are so many minor values, and so many of them are in core vocabulary, that it may be wise to consider them as unpredictable. Whenever someone wants to give examples to substantiate a claim that English spelling is chaotic, they always use words with 'ou' and 'ow'!

**5.5
Teaching
suggestions**

Here are a few exercises that can be used to help learners consolidate or discover some of the sound/spelling rules.

The values of 'c' (see Table 2 page 102)

Give the learners the following two lists of words. Ask them to read the word aloud. When it has been established that 'c' can have two values, ask if they can see what the rule is. Prompt them to 'look at the letter that follows' if necessary.

List A		*List B*	
cell	certain	cat	catch
place	dance	cup	coffee
city	cycle	cry	coin
policy	cent	call	cake
decide	cinema	came	cost
		custom	could

The two 'ch' values (See Table 4 page 103)

(either /k/ 'chord' or /tʃ/ 'cheap' initially and only /tʃ/ 'each' finally)
Give the learners the following nonsense words. Which of these have two possible pronunciations and which have only one?

chiep chup poch meech chint neach choon chiln ach neach
chen choad milch

One-value composite consonants (See Table 4 page 103)

(ck ng tch le qu wh ph sh)
Read aloud a list of words to the learners, such as the following:

queen quit prolong ringlet mock black photograph whip when
stretch wheat whole Dutch epitaph usher shop cash equip able

Ask the learners to count the number of sounds they hear for each word. Then show them a written list and ask them to show what letters stand for each sound, thus:

1   2   3
m   a   tch

Position constraints on one-value composite consonants (see Table 4 page 103)

Look at these nonsense words – which could be English words and which break the rules of English spelling?

miqu lowh meewh whipson whaply whoy thock queep shasting
plick ckall nequilt nooqu atcho tchert fitch phit upsiph ling
ngup ngurt mang nong phatter

A variant of this use of nonsense words is a Scrabble-type activity. Learners are given random sets of cards or blocks with single vowel letters, digraphs, composite letters (say, two vowels and three consonants), and arrange them if possible into a real or possible English word.

The silent e rule (See Table 5 page 104)

To demonstrate this rule learners are given the following pairs of words for oral practice: cut/cute, pip/pipe, mat/mate, fin/fine, etc. Next they are given only one member of the pair, and have to pronounce the other member: us (use), hope (hop), etc.

Single vowel letters in polysyllabic words (see page 105)

Step One: Using a list of words with the vowel letters 'a, e, o, and u' in the stressed syllable, establish whether the letters have their short, or name value, by reading aloud and placing them in a grid like the one below:

	a	*e*	*o*	*u*
name value	relation	completion	explosion	confusion
short value	action	collection	option	discussion

Step Two: For each word, mark off the suffix and indicate the stress pattern:

o O o   O o
re lat/-tion   act/-ion

Step Three: Get the students to count the number of consonants following the stressed vowel. Point out the rule (one consonant – name value; two consonants – short value). See if *they* can spot the pattern, instead of providing it.

Step Four: Point out that the rule works for suffixes with i – vowel and give several examples.

Step Five: Give several words with the letter 'i' to show that this rule does not work for 'i'. (politician/permission/delicious/initial/subscription/vision, etc.)

Crosswords

Crossword puzzles are very useful for providing a focus on spelling. Of course they must be suited to the learners in the target words, nature of the clues, etc. Partially completed puzzles can be less daunting. Learners can also devise their own simple puzzles – they can make up a personal puzzle (with words that refer to them and their likes/dislikes) or a puzzle can be constructed around a particular area of vocabulary. Students can exchange and complete each other's puzzles. Mistakes due to spelling should be treated as a matter of interest and discussion.

References

1 S. Schane 'Linguistics, Spelling and Pronunciation' (*TESOL Quarterly* 6 1972).

2 C. Kreidler 'Teaching English Spelling and Pronunciation' (*TESOL Quarterly* 6 1972).

3 Sources of these errors are: R. Nash 'Orthographic Interference in Pronunciation' in Nash (ed) *Readings in Spanish–English Linguistics* (Inter-American University Press 1978); John Bird, Eurocentre, Forest Hill, London; my own students.

4 These rules are based on R. Venezky *The Structure of English Orthography* (Mouton 1970).

5 W. Dickerson 'English Orthography – A Guide to Stress and Vowel Quality' (*International Review of Applied Linguistics* xvi/2 1978).

6

Integrated pronunciation teaching

What is meant by 'integrated pronunciation teaching'? Many teachers will have slightly different criteria, but most would agree about what it is not. If you decided 'not-to-integrate' you would give lessons, or slots of lessons, in which work was done on sounds, rhythm, or intonation, for example. Then, assuming that your points had been made, sounds had been practised, and so on, you would pay no more attention to matters of pronunciation in any other lessons or learning activity.

Most teachers would reject this way of working because it is clearly artificial and unworkable. It is impossible to restrict pronunciation work to particular lessons or slots. Whenever a new word is met in a text, learners will ask how it is pronounced; when a learner says something and the teacher and/or class members don't understand, the intended word has to be discovered and its correct pronunciation presented; when learners are listening to taped material and misinterpret a speaker's intentions because they have missed some feature of stress or intonation, the teacher must draw their attention to it. There is, therefore, an inevitability about pronunciation work and there is an argument that if pronunciation is so often *a part of* many language learning activities then it is automatically 'integrated'. It is possible to state the case even more extremely: *whenever* learners *hear* English or try to speak themselves they are 'doing pronunciation work'; every lesson is a pronunciation lesson; every time the teacher speaks he or she is presenting a spoken model.

Clearly we must discount this last claim because of what we know about sounds as the medium for the expression of meanings. When we speak, our very conscious concern is to get our message across – we don't pay conscious attention to what our lips, tongue and jaw are doing or the way we are using voice pitch. The same is true when we listen. Unless the speaker has a speech impediment or a strange voice quality, we don't pay conscious attention to the way they are making sounds. If we start to do so we may even 'tune out' enough to miss parts of their message.

But even if we reject the extreme argument, doesn't the fact that pronunciation will so often be a part of language learning activities mean that we really don't have to worry about integration? In one limited sense, yes. It is simply impossible to avoid pronunciation work, unless learners are only learning to read English (silently). But if the goal of integration is set because it is believed that this leads to more effective and efficient learning (and this is a commonly held assumption) then two vital factors are missing from this definition of 'integration'.

The first factor has to do with the consistency and planning that is associated with integration. If the teacher, for example, corrects mispronunciations whenever they occur, then he or she still can't be sure that those corrections will cumulatively lead to 'better pronunciation'. The teacher may end up spending just as much time correcting features which are not crucial for intelligibility as correcting those that are. Also, the teacher may end up working only on those points that lend themselves to on-the-spot treatment. If it seems that a point on, say, linkage or rhythm will take too much time to treat and will disrupt the course of the lesson, then the teacher may let these pass. These may be the very features which affect the learner's intelligibility.

The second factor relates to the learner. No matter how much teachers work towards integration in their teaching, unless the learners themselves, as a result of this, integrate pronunciation into their *learning*, then little success or positive change can be expected. Learners must be encouraged to accept the role of 'self-monitor' – to bring their pronunciation under control, always to be on the look-out for the way words are pronounced or for the way English people use their voices. The teacher must approach pronunciation in such a way that it encourages appropriate attitudes in learners and helps them to give the necessary time and effort to it. With these points in mind, let us look at some ways to achieve this kind of integration.

6.1 Pronunciation and vocabulary work

In the preparation of lessons teachers go through a process of deciding at what levels they are going to exploit materials. For example, in preparing a listening activity the teacher will note the words/phrases that may be unfamiliar to learners and decide how to treat these items – whether to wait for learners to ask their meaning, to have a vocabulary presentation stage, to design a pre-activity to focus on the new vocabulary or a post-activity to consolidate and practise the newly learned words. No matter what type of work is being done at the level of vocabulary, it presents the teacher with opportunities for work on the pronunciation of words. In particular there are several aspects of pronunciation that can be easily integrated into vocabulary work: sounds, stress pattern, linkage and simplifications, sound/spelling correspondences, and clusters of sounds.

The sounds of words

It goes without saying that the sounds that make up the word should be an area of focus. If the teacher has made each learner aware of his or her particular sound priorities, then the teacher can simply ask each learner to check whether the new word has any of their 'priority sounds'. A few seconds of practice and experimentation with pronouncing the word(s) can be carried out as appropriate.

The stress patterns of words

As we have seen, the stress pattern of a word is as much a part of its identity as its constituent sounds. Whenever a new word is encountered learners should make learning the stress pattern part of learning the word. Learners should be encouraged to keep vocabulary lists with stress marked on the words and the strong vowel circled. This habit can be positively encouraged by doing this with them at the end of each unit in their coursebook. If the coursebook has unit vocabulary lists or glossaries, then the words can be marked there. If these are not provided, then the lists can be prepared in class as a joint exercise, with the students selecting which words should be in the list and then referring to a dictionary or listening to the teacher's model to remind them what stress pattern the word has. It may also be appropriate for learners to add a column of 'related forms' to their list. This column will contain words with prefixes/suffixes with their stress pattern marked. If word stress rules have been presented, then there is an opportunity for consolidation in the preparation of these lists.

Linkage and sound simplifications

It is quite difficult for learners to remember to use linkage in their speech. First of all, if they are reading aloud, or using written language as a stimulus for oral production, there is no 'visual reminder' of linkage. Secondly, as we have seen there are specific rules for linkage. Not all words in a phrase/clause undergo linkage – it depends on what sounds get placed next to each other. Consequently, these are very difficult rules for learners to put into practice.

One strategy which will help learners to use linkage is available to teachers when working at the level of vocabulary. When phrases or groups of words which co-occur frequently are met, treat these as *units*, and draw learners' attention to the pronunciation of the unit. For example, let's say you have been working on 'since/ago'. In work on the latter, phrases such as 'five days ago, two weeks ago, many years ago' will crop up. When the 'a' of 'ago' is preceded by an 's' (as it often will be) there is a smooth transition between the 's' and the vowel. Draw learners' attention to this, using the tie notation mentioned in Chapter 3. Do a few seconds of choral or individual practice. There are many opportunities to look at groups of words or phrases and the linkage involved in their pronunciation: idioms, compound words, proper names and titles, phrases such as 'as well as', 'not only', 'in place of', and parts of the verb phrases ('must have, could have, be‿able', etc.) are just a few possibilities.

Sound/spelling correspondences

When written materials are being used the teacher can help the learners develop and consolidate their knowledge of spelling rules by asking them if they can figure out the pronunciation of a new word from its spelling. As was emphasized in Chapter 5, the teacher should praise 'good' guesses, ones that show an awareness of the spelling conventions even if the word in question happens to have an exceptional spelling. The converse strategy can be used when new words are heard for the first time. The teacher can ask: 'How do you think it might be spelled?' If several versions are suggested their merits and demerits can be discussed before the actual spelling is given. Of course it's unwise to treat every new word in this way. Criteria for selection might well include: (1) the existence of a cognate word in the native language; (2) words that are particularly important for particular learners (for example, learners of English for Specific Purposes); (3) words that have an exceptional spelling.

Clusters

Clusters in a word or sequences of consonants can lead to a variety of coping strategies from learners. These can also be consistently tackled during vocabulary focus stages of lessons.

Two different approaches can be used to do work on the consonant clusters and sequences that occur in vocabulary which is being presented or practised. The teacher can focus on those clusters which are difficult for particular language groups, or on the way English speakers deal with clusters and sequences of consonants. Again, if learners are aware of their 'sound priorities' they can be asked to check new words for their problematic sequences. An example of the second strategy would be to draw learners' attention to the way English speakers pronounce sequences and clusters, especially when the learners might be easily misled by the spelling. For example, in meeting the word 'blanket' learners may not realize that the 'n' is pronounced as a /ŋ/ as in 'sing'. (The presence of the 'k' triggers off this pronunciation.) It's best to introduce these features gradually, rather than try to present general rules.

**6.2
Exploiting transcriptions of recorded material**

The teacher can go a long way towards integrating pronunciation work into the teaching programme by devising ways to work with the transcripts of dialogues/monologues and so on that are provided in coursebooks and teaching materials. These transcripts can be used for work on weak forms, rhythm, aspects of connected speech, intonation, etc. in a variety of ways. The two basic approaches are *marking* activities, in which learners listen to the spoken material and use symbols or other conventions to indicate aspects of pronunciation, and *scripting* activities, in which learners first read the transcript and predict or specify certain features of pronunciation and then listen to the taped material. Below are a few suggestions.

6.2.1
Marking activities

Marking transcripts for weak forms

Learners have the transcript of a text, and as the tape is played they listen for weak forms. The tape is played as many times as necessary. Some learners may need a suggested method of working, such as 'check each little word', or they could be given a pre-selected list of words to check. Conversely, learners could be asked to listen for full forms of a pre-selected list of words. Of course the teacher should make sure that there are some to be found! But even if there are none, setting such a task is an effective way to reinforce the scarcity of full forms in conversational speech. If materials contain a dialogue in which a word occurs in both its full and weak forms, this can be an especially appropriate task to set.

Marking for rhythm

Using their transcripts learners can mark the rhythm they hear in terms of stress and unstress. There will of course be a correlation between words marked as unstressed and weak forms. One useful task is to ask learners to mark unstressed syllables only; this will remind them of how many unstressed syllables can occur together in some utterances. Different coloured pens for stress and unstress, especially those which can be drawn across the print without obscuring the words, are particularly useful. Learners can also be set the task of first reading the transcript before they hear the recording and predicting the occurrence of weak forms and stress and unstress, and then listening to the material to check if they guessed correctly.

6.2.2
Scripting activities

In asking learners to predict the occurrences of weak forms and stress and unstress the task becomes one of preparing a script. This can be developed into a genuine scripting activity in which learners *impose* their own interpretation upon a particular text. These scripted texts can be:

— compared with each other
— checked against a tape or video recording
— used to elicit particular 'readings' from others.

If the scripts are heavily marked, then probably only the teacher will be able to perform in accordance with the notations. If only one or two features have been scripted, then learners themselves can have a go at 'performing' in accordance with each others' scripts. Advanced students may find it interesting to script for all sorts of dimensions such as emotions, speed, or volume, and the activity can be compared to 'directing a play'.

Once learners become familiar with these two activities, then they can easily be introduced into lessons. Needless to say, they shouldn't become an obligatory part of each and every encounter with a transcript! The teacher can choose to treat one or two lines only in this way, or select particularly interesting sections of a dialogue. It's very much a matter of the teacher 'being alive' to the possibilities for pronunciation points in teaching materials, of 'finding the opportunities'.

One point about the use of intonation-marking conventions. It is often assumed that learners can cope quite happily with lines indicating intonation. This is certainly demonstrated by the widespread use of such marks in intonation materials. This is not so. Some learners find it extremely difficult to follow the wavy lines. The teacher should monitor this carefully. It's best to keep the indication of pitch as simple as possible – for example, arrows can be put at the beginning of a clause or rising-falling straight lines across the text to indicate general direction of pitch.

6.3
**Integrating
intonation**

Intonation is such a complex aspect of spoken language that it is particularly important that the teacher calls the learners' attention to the use of intonation when they are listening, and comments on their use of it when speaking. This is best done by the use of probing questions which refer to functions of intonation already presented. For example, if a learner replies to an information question with a rising pitch, the teacher might pause and ask: 'Are you sure?'; or, to a learner who has used very little pitch movement, the teacher might say: 'You sound a bit bored.' When a tag question appears in a text, the teacher might stop the tape and ask: 'What answer does the speaker expect?'. Keeping learners constantly 'alive' to the use of intonation is one way to ensure that this aspect of language is well integrated into lessons.

6.4
The role of self-evaluation and monitoring

In the early stages of learning, learners are dependent on the teacher for information about the critical sounds of English and for feedback on their performance. At this stage they cannot be expected to know which features are important and which are not, and what sound contrasts need to be made. But as their exposure to English increases, and as they acquire the necessary discriminatory skills, learners begin to develop their own 'internal' criteria of what is acceptable and what is not.

Of course it is impossible to predict exactly when learners can begin to be less dependent on the teacher for feedback, but a good indicator is *self-correction*. When a learner begins to spontaneously correct his/her own performance, then this is a sure sign of the development of self-evaluation and monitoring skills.

Teachers must find ways to tap these developing skills, for unless learners develop the ability to monitor their own speech and make this a habit, then the possibility of change or adjustments in pronunciation will be blocked. Evaluating someone else's pronunciation is a skill which needs conscious effort and practice, as all teachers know; it is even more difficult to monitor one's own speech. The pressures of speaking – choosing what to say, finding the words, finding the appropriate grammatical structures – leave little mental energy for paying attention to how the sounds come out. So learners need suggested strategies, and opportunities to practise these strategies, to improve in this area. One way of helping them is to make acts of monitoring and self-evaluation an integral part of work both inside and outside the classroom. We will look at three ways of doing this.

6.4.1
The instant or action replay techniques

Language teachers often feel themselves to be in a dilemma when it comes to intervening to correct poor pronunciation. The last thing one wants to do is to interrupt learners in the full flow of speech, especially when they are involved in some kind of communication activity. One way of avoiding disruptive interventions and still providing for the development of self-evaluation and monitoring skills is to use 'action' or 'instant' replay. These terms are of course taken from televised sports coverage – with the technology now available one can show an instant replay of a crucial goal or point, even during a live broadcast. In the language classroom, 'replay' can take two forms:

(a) A tape recording can be made while the learners are involved in a speaking activity (a role play, a discussion, a communication game, etc.). At the end of the activity, or at the end of a stage in an activity, the learners can listen to themselves on tape and evaluate their own speech. In this case, the 'replay' is an instant taped replay which provides immediate feedback for the learners.

(b) When some kind of speaking activity has been done in the lesson, the teacher can ask for an 'action replay'. The learners are asked to repeat the activity and this time to pay more attention to their pronunciation. The teacher can either give the blanket instruction 'go for a better pronunciation', or be selective and ask the learners to attend to specific areas such as weak forms, the use of pitch range, or 'problem sounds'. This latter more focused approach is probably the one teachers should use most often, but learners will eventually be able to make a series of adjustments which will amount to them 'putting on their best pronunciation'. This technique is probably best used for short exchanges or chunks of speech. You can't ask learners to action-replay a whole discussion. It has the important advantage that, having done the speaking task or part of it *once*, the learners have already decided *what* to say. In the action replay there is more mental energy available for self-monitoring. This type of technique will ensure that self-monitoring and evaluation skills are developed. Furthermore, the fact that they know there will be regular opportunities for paying careful attention to the way they speak, means that learners can also relax during certain other speaking activities and use a style of pronunciation that they know is adequate for communication when the conditions are most favourable (when they have a patient, tolerant, interested audience). This will not only help over-anxious learners to relax, but will make all learners aware that it is quite normal to have more than one style of speaking.

It cannot be repeated too often that learners cannot be expected to 'do everything' at the same time in pronunciation. This is why one so often finds that when asked to produce a sound or feature 'on demand' learners do it perfectly, but immediately return to a poorer production when they speak spontaneously. With the teacher's help the learner should work out a set of points to focus on. This may be a list of three to four problem sounds and general attention to an area such as weak forms. It is to these points that the teacher should devote most attention in the evaluation and comment phases of instant or action replay sessions.

6.4.2
Oral homework[1]

Once learners have become familiar with self-monitoring and self-evaluation activities in the classroom, they can be introduced to the idea of 'oral homework', that is, homework which involves oral production instead of written or reading assignments. Assignments are prepared, rehearsed, and then recorded on video or audio tape, either during sessions set aside for private study or at home. Learners evaluate their own performance using a scoring system specified by the teacher. There is then an opportunity for feedback and evaluation by the teacher. This may be given during 'pronunciation clinics' (ten or fifteen minute slots when students can discuss their assignments) or during a lesson in which class members have the opportunity to play or show their completed assignments and receive comments from their teacher and colleagues.

It is important that there is a variety of oral homework assignments. Here are some possibilities.

Describing tasks

(a) *What's the difference?* Learners are given pictures of two partially similar objects or scenes, two cars, two items of clothing, etc. They must describe the differences between them.

(b) *Describe a place*. Learners can describe a place that is familiar to them, or be given a picture cue.

(c) *Describe a person*. Task set as in (b).

(d) *Describe a personal experience*: a dream, a family celebration, a ceremony, the last time you were in hospital, a sports or entertainment event, etc.

(e) *What can you see*? Learners are told to imagine themselves in a particular place, and have to describe what is in their field of vision.

Speculation tasks

(a) *What happened next*? Learners are given a photograph showing some sort of action, situation, etc. which is about to change drastically, for example two cars on a collision course. They have to describe what happened next, or is about to happen.

(b) *The other half*. Learners are given a photograph or picture that has been torn in half. They must speculate about what might be in the rest of the photograph.

(c) *What is it part of*? Learners are given a close-up photograph of part of a large object or a small piece of some object. They must describe it and suggest what it might be part of.

(d) *What would you do*? Learners state their course of action, or a solution to a problem.

State your opinion

(a) Learners are provided with a written statement on a controversial topic. They must react to it by agreeing or disagreeing and give reasons.

(b) *State your preference*. Prompts are different examples of the same item, – two rooms, two restaurant menus, two pictures of holiday resorts, etc. Their task is to say which they prefer and why.

Giving directions/instructions

This can range from a task such as starting a car to getting from home to English class, etc.

Social graces

Learners are given a brief description of a specific situation – the well-known formula: 'You are . . . What would you do?/say?'

Story-telling tasks

Prompts can be strip cartoons, or learners can give a plot summary of a film or programme they've seen or a book they've read.

Many of the above suggestions will be familiar as classroom activities. In giving these as 'oral homework assignments', it is important to remember that learners will need some guidelines to follow and an indication of what is expected of them. Learners at the lower levels of proficiency should be given those assignments which have a lot of 'external support'. A series of questions to be answered can be helpful for the describing tasks, or photograph cues can be numbered to give learners a guide as to the order of their points.

Several of these taped assignments can form the basis of classroom activities. For example, all the responses to 'State your opinion' tasks can be listened to, the results tabulated, tendencies identified, and reasons for these discussed. 'What can you see?' can form the basis for a classroom activity in which the whole class listens to the description and tries to figure out where the speaker was. For the directions tasks, the class must listen and try to follow the directions. For 'The other half' the class could be shown the missing halves of the photographs and try to decide who had which other half. One of the clear advantages of using recordings in these ways is that it will give the learners a context for the task and a clear purpose for speaking. This is an aspect which is often missing from oral practice. The fact that a record exists of the speech means that it is easier for teacher and classmates to note and comment on points of pronunciation. Oral homework tasks exploited in this way resemble the instant replay techniques described above.

A good way to introduce the notion of oral homework is to build a lesson around the oral assignments (or indeed any taped production) of a group of learners unknown to the students. This will help the learners to:

— realize that they do have the ability to evaluate performance
— get them used to any scoring system that will be used
— acquaint them with the type of assignments which will be given
— acquaint them with the operation of the equipment they will be using.

The recording of these assignments can be done on the 'student's tape'.

6.4.3

Keeping a record of progress – the student's tape

Language learning is an extended process, and whenever we are involved in a learning task over a long period of time it is very easy to lose track of our progress. The conviction 'I must be getting better at this' is often not enough to sustain motivation and effort. In any complex learning task, learners need feedback – they need to know what they have accomplished and what they still have to do. It is equally important that learners feel that attention is being paid to their progress, and that they are indeed progressing. The student's tape is one way to provide this record of progress.

Each student is given a tape at the beginning of his or her period of study. For non-beginners the first sample recorded can be the diagnostic exercises done on arrival – perhaps those carried out as a check on intelligibility (see Chapter 2). At regular intervals similar samples are recorded. Students can also use the tape to record oral homework assignments. The tape can form the basis of individual 'pronunciation clinics' with the teacher, or workshops with a very small number of students which may be part of a consultation period. Learners will know that the teacher will be working with the whole class on certain general priority areas, but it is vital that students feel that their individual problems are being catered for. These sessions in which the teacher spends a few minutes listening to the student's tape, playing earlier and later sequences and analysing whether 'problem x' is still a problem, are extremely valuable to learners. And if 'problem x' hasn't changed, then the teacher might discuss with the student whether or not this is serious.

This individual attention will be interpreted by the learner as another reflection of the teacher's concern for his or her pronunciation. If the teacher's concern is obvious, then the learner's own concern and motivation will be positively affected.[2]

6.5 Opportunities to excel

Learners should also be involved occasionally in activities which require them to 'put on their best pronunciation' – activities involving planning, rehearsal and presentation.

Voice-overs

For example, students can be asked to prepare a 'voice-over' for a short video or film sequence. The 'voice-over' is a common feature of news broadcasts, documentary films, current events programmes, etc. Viewers see a sequence of images and the voice-over tells them about what they are seeing. The activity can be organized in the following way.

Students are given a short film or video sequence, and, if necessary, notes about what should be included in the narration. They write the script and then rehearse it so that it is synchronized with the visual images. They may need a few tries at this and may need to shorten or lengthen their script. They record and re-record until they are satisfied with their delivery and pronunciation. Then the sequence is presented to the class. In doing this task the learners should try to achieve the best pronunciation they can.[3]

If film or video-taped material is not available, then learners can prepare a 'slide commentary' or give a demonstration of a skill (for example, preparing a national dish) and give a running commentary. All these presentations should be seen as opportunities to use their best pronunciation and to demonstrate their skills as speakers.

References

1 This is a development of an idea of teachers at Eurocentre, Bournemouth.
2 See G. Brown and G. Yule *Teaching the Spoken Language* (Cambridge University Press, 1983) for a similar discussion of the use of the student's tape.
3 Such materials have been prepared by the BBC ('Television English'). Information can be obtained from Bush House, London WC2B 4PH.

Part two

Using part two

In the following sections on individual languages, the differences between the pronunciation of English and the language are discussed in terms of the problems learners tend to have. The comments under the heading Learner Strategies (LS) describe the ways learners tend to cope, for example by substituting one sound for another or misplacing stress in certain words. Of course, these are *tendencies* – not all learners will invariably use these strategies. The comments under Teacher Strategies (TS) give ways teachers can help – correction techniques, teaching suggestions and so on.

Priorities

Some problems learners have need to be given *high priority* because they are vital for intelligibility; others do not affect intelligibility and can be given *low priority* (for example, sounds which occur relatively rarely in English, such as the /ʒ/ in 'treaʃure'). Learners may also have problems which can be given *optional attention*. These are features which, although they may contribute to a very noticeable foreign accent, will usually not lead to intelligibility problems because:

1 native listeners are generally used to these features of foreign accents, or
2 there are regional accents or varieties of English that use the particular feature so it is familiar to English ears, or
3 the feature is 'close enough' to the native feature (see discussion in Chapter 2), or
4 relatively few words are kept apart by the feature or sound.

Whether attention is given to these OA features or not will depend on whether the teacher assesses a need for improvement or whether the learner *wants* to aim for a near-native pronunciation.

These priorities are indicated by HP, LP, or OA in the left margin opposite the description of the problem.

In general, the areas of rhythm, word stress, and sentence stress are *high priority* areas for *all learners*.

It is difficult to give priorities for intonation unless one is able to predict what kinds of conversational encounters the learner will be involved in. For example, for a learner who will use English in very formal settings, with listeners of 'higher status', the intonation associated with politeness and mitigation is a high priority (see discussion in Chapter 4). The points on intonation are designed to give the teacher an indication of what might be potential 'trouble spots'.

Note: In the case of the two 'th' sounds, *two* codes are necessary. For content words in stressed position, /ð/ and /θ/ should be given HP; but for function words ('the, this, that', etc.) OA is appropriate – pronunciations such as 'ze' for '*the*' or 'dat' for '*that*' tend not to affect intelligibility, but 'sick' for '*thick*' will lead to confusion.

Arabic

Rhythm
HP

Arabic is a stress-timed language, so Arab learners will not have as many problems in this area as, say, French speakers have. But there is a difference in the comparative force of pronunciation of stressed and unstressed syllables in English and Arabic. In English, there is a great difference in force: unstressed syllables can be pronounced very weakly and may almost disappear; stressed syllables can be very explicitly and fully pronounced. In Arabic, the difference in the force of pronunciation of stressed and unstressed syllables is not nearly so extreme: an unstressed syllable can have a full vowel and be pronounced fairly clearly. So the difference in the rhythmic patterns of Arabic and English is a difference in degree, not in kind. Although both Arabic and English have a stress-timed rhythm, Arab learners still have difficulties.

Sentence stress
HP

Sentence stress in Arabic is similar to that in English; 'content' words are usually stressed and grammatical or 'function' words are usually unstressed. However, there are two differences which can lead to problems:

1 Function words in Arabic do not have two forms – vowels in words in unstressed position keep their 'full' value, unlike vowels in unstressed words in English, which are reduced to 'schwa'.
2 Verb phrases do not occur in Arabic (compare English 'can do', 'have done', 'should have done', etc.).

LS Because of the above differences watch out for errors such as the following:
— use of full forms of pronouns. The learner will sound as if he or she is making a contrast when this is not the intention.
— use of full forms of auxiliary verbs when the weak form should be used. ('I can do it' instead of 'I can (kən) do it'.) It will sound as if the speaker is protesting or denying a previous statement ('I can do it even though you say I can't) when this meaning is not intended.

Contrastive stress
HP

In order to show strong contrast, Arabic uses word order (the relevant word or phrase is moved to the beginning of the sentence) so learners will be unfamiliar with the use of stress to show contrast as in English.

Word stress
HP

Polysyllabic Arabic words do have stressed and unstressed syllables, so learners will have no trouble with the notion that stress is allocated to a particular syllable in an English word. Nor will there be total unfamiliarity with the notion of stress shift.

LS In Arabic, placement of stress in words is determined by the number and order of consonants and by the quality of the vowel. In particular, learners tend to transfer three of their mother-tongue habits to English. Watch out for:

— learners putting stress on the final syllable of English words ending in a vowel followed by two consonants, as in 'difficult', 'comfort' and 'expert'.

— a tendency in learners to place stress on endings such as '-est', '-ism', '-less' and '-ness' (because of the above -VCC rule).

— learners putting stress on the last syllable of a word ending in a diphthong or a long vowel plus a single consonant, as in 'irritate', 'gratitude', and 'institute'.

Linkage in connected speech
OA

Arabic does not have linking glides and uses glottal stops to separate vowel from vowel, and vowel from consonant in consecutive words. Also, in Arabic no word begins with a vowel – a glottal stop always precedes the vowel.

Consonant clusters and sequences
HP

English permits longer consonant clusters and sequences than Arabic does. The main difficulty for learners is three-element clusters initially and finally, as in 'street' and 'against'.

Although two-element clusters at the beginning of words seem to cause fewer problems, those beginning with 's' are particularly difficult ('speak', 'state').

LS The learner will tend to insert a vowel to break up the groups of consonants. For example, instead of pronouncing s-k-t in 'asked', this will be pronounced as a two-syllable word (as-ked) and, similarly, 'against' will become 'again-est'.

Problems with vowels

English has many more vowels than Arabic. As a result, learners will tend to use their relatively small number of vowels to 'cover' the larger English vowel system.

HP

1 /ɪ/ as in 'bɪt' and /ɛ/ as in 'bɛt' confusion.

HP

2 /ɛ/ as in 'bɛt', /a/ as in 'hat', or /ʌ/ as in 'bʌt' are confused. There may be problems distinguishing sets like 'pit/pat/putt', 'cut/cat', etc.

HP

3 The caught/coat contrast can be extremely troublesome (/ɔ/ vs. /ou/).

LS Learners may tend to use their /o/ sound for both.

TS To help learners achieve the /ɔ/ vowel, use the Arabic word for 'fashion', /mo:da/. The vowel in this word is very close to the English vowel in 'caught', 'bought', etc.

LP

4 The Arabic vowel system has no diphthongs, but these seem rarely to cause problems.

Note: The schwa vowel does occur in Arabic in unstressed syllables, as in the first syllable of the name 'Mohammed'. Learners may still have problems with this vowel because in English it can be represented by many different vowel letters. This is in contrast to Arabic orthographic conventions, which adhere very much to the convention 'one sound–one letter'.

Problems with consonants

Consonants which occur in English but not in Arabic

HP

1 /p/ as in 'pat'.

LS Arabic speakers tend to produce the sound /p/ without aspiration. To English ears, this will sound more like a /b/ than a /p/.

TS See 4.3.3.

HP/OA

2 /θ/ as in 'thick' and /ð/ as in 'that'.

LS Learners will tend to substitute /s/ for /θ/ and /z/ for /ð/.

TS See 4.3.3.

HP

3 /tʃ/ as in 'chip'.
Although Arabic does not have /tʃ/, it does have a /t/ sound, and a /ʃ/ sound. Since /tʃ/ is really a combination of these two, it may not be difficult for learners to achieve the sound.

LP

4 /dʒ/ as in 'junk'.

LS Learners will confuse /dʒ/ as in 'junk' with /ʒ/ as in 'pleasure' or /tʃ/ in 'chip' (if they can make the latter).

Sounds which are slightly different in Arabic and English

LP

5 Arabic /l/ is very 'clear' in quality. It is made with the tip of the tongue and resembles the /l/ Welsh and Irish speakers use.

LP

6 Arab learners will tend to use their native /r/ when speaking English – this is a 'trilled' or 'rolled' type of /r/.

LP

7 In words like 'sing', 'ring', etc. Arab learners will tend to pronounce the /g/ as a separate sound, instead of using just the nasal sound (/ŋ/) as most, but not all, English speakers do.

Intonation

Arabic speakers tend to have relatively minor difficulties with intonation. There are some noticeable differences:

1 In Arabic, there is what might be called 'sustained pitch', that is, the pitch of the voice stays steady on each syllable, and then the speaker jumps up or down in pitch for the next syllable. In English, the pitch tends to change or waver on syllables. So, whereas Arabic pitch patterns might be compared to a flight of stairs, English patterns are smoother, more like an escalator.

2 Arabic tends to use a narrower range of falling pitch over the phrase or clause. To the English ear, this may be interpreted as a lack of the

correct completion signal (the 'vocal full stop' at the end of a clause) and may give an impression of 'inconclusiveness'.

Of these two features, only 2 merits attention.

Sources Yowel Y. Aziz 'Some Problems of English Word Stress for the Iraqi Learner' (*English Language Teaching* XXXIV/2, 1980).
Mohammed Helmy Heleil 'A brief contrastive phonological analysis of Egyptian Arabic and English' (unpublished M. Litt. thesis University of Edinburgh 1972).

Chinese

There are many varieties of Chinese. These comments refer to the Cantonese variety (spoken in Hong Kong) and the Hokkien variety (spoken by a large number of Singaporean Chinese). Many of the problems are shared, but differences are pointed out where appropriate (H stands for Hokkien and C for Cantonese).

Problems with consonants

HP

1 The sounds /p, t, k, m, n/ and the sound /ŋ/ as in 'si*ng*' in final position.

The above six sounds exist in C and H, but when they occur at the end of a syllable they are never 'released', i.e. for /p/ and /m/ the lips remain closed; for /t/ and /n/ the tongue tip clings to the roof of the mouth; and for /k/ and /ŋ/ the back of the tongue clings to the roof of the mouth. Chinese speakers will transfer these articulatory habits to English, and consequently these sounds seem to be 'swallowed' and the English listener may have difficulty hearing which sound was produced. (This is so even though English speakers themselves occasionally do not release these sounds at the ends of words.)

HP/OA

2 Chinese does not have either of the 'th' sounds.

LS Learners will substitute either /t/ or /f/ for /θ/ as in '*th*ick' and either /d/ or /v/ for /ð/ as in '*th*is'. /f/ and /v/ substitutes cause more problems.

HP

3 C does not have /v/ as in '*v*an' although /f/ as in '*f*an' does occur.

LS At the end of a word learners tend to substitute /f/ for /v/, so 'save' will sound like 'safe'.
At the beginning of a word learners tend to substitute /w/ for /v/, so 'vine' will sound like 'wine'. H speakers may show confusion with /b/ or /p/.

LP

4 Although /tʃ/ as in '*ch*ur*ch*' does occur in Chinese (the name 'Choy') /dʒ/ does not, so learners will not be able to distinguish or produce a difference between 'Choy' and 'joy' (initial position) or 'rich' and 'ridge' (final position).

HP

5 Although /b, d, g/ occur at the beginning of words in C and H, they do not occur at the ends of words.

LS Learners will tend to substitute /p, t, k/. However, these are not very adequate substitutes for the reasons stated in 1 above.

HP

6 Chinese has /s/ but no /z/.
LS /ʃ/ as in '*sh*e' is a common substitution for /z/. Practice will be needed in both initial and final position.

HP

7 /ʃ/ as in 'she' does not exist as a separate sound in Chinese.

LS Learners will commonly substitute /s/ for this sound, so pairs like 'see' and 'she', 'same' and 'shame' will be problematic. This situation is complicated by the fact that before the /u/ sound as in 'moon' learners will substitute /ʃ/ for /s/, so they will pronounce 'Sue' as 'shoe'. This is because /ʃ/ is a variant of the /s/ sound before this particular vowel. The problem is not making the sound /ʃ/, but what sound comes next.

TS /ʃ/ does exist in Mandarin Chinese, so if learners are familiar with Mandarin it may help to mention this (but it will probably not help the problem before the vowel /u/).

LP

8 /ʒ/ as in 'rouge' does not exist in Chinese.

HP

9 Confusion between /l/ and /r/.
There is a well-known perceptual confusion between these two sounds, and a production difficulty.

LS Learners have a tendency to use a sound which sounds most like an /r/ to the English ear for both sounds:

'all' may sound like 'or'
'fell' may sound like 'fear'
'fall' may sound like 'four'

but in initial position an /l/-like sound is often substituted for /r/:

'ride' may sound like 'lied'
'raid' may sound like 'laid'

The same problems occur when these two sounds are grouped with other sounds in a sequence or a cluster:

'blue' may sound like 'brew'
'flight' may sound like 'fright'
'clutch' may sound like 'crutch'

HP

10 /n/ and /l/ confusion.
Some Chinese speakers may have difficulties perceiving and producing these sounds before vowels.

HP

11 /t/ and /d/ confusion ('town – down').
This is a problem for H speakers, who will not use enough aspiration for /t/.

Problems with vowels
HP

1 /i/ as in eat /ɪ/ as in 'it'. Both these vowel sounds occur in Chinese, but there are restrictions on which consonants can follow them. Learners may have no trouble with the words 'sick', 'ring', 'king' or 'lip' but with other following consonants there may be difficulties (for example, 'fill', 'sit', 'did', 'dim').

HP

2 /ei/ and /ɛ/ ('mate – met').

LS Learners will have no problems pronouncing this diphthong when it is the last sound in a word, as in 'lay', 'say', etc., but when it is followed by a consonant, they may tend to substitute /ɛ/ as in 'bed'.

HP

3 /ɑ/–/ʌ/–/ɔ/ ('hard–but–caught').
Both H and C speakers may have problems distinguishing these vowels.

4 Chinese has a vowel which is very close to English schwa. This sound can be used as an adequate substitute for schwa. An example word with this sound is 'seun' /sən/ ('believe').

HP

5 /ou/ as in 'coat' is present in C but not in H.
H learners may have problems, and C speakers may have difficulty distinguishing it from /au/ as in 'now'.

OA

6 Chinese learners will have problems distinguishing /u/ as in 'shoot' from /ʊ/ as in 'book'. These sounds are variants of one another in Chinese, so this is a very tricky area for learners.

TS Perception and production practice with pairs such as:

suit	soot
cooed	could
wooed	would
fool	full

Rhythm and stress
HP

All aspects of rhythm and stress, including word stress, are highly problematical for learners and must be given *high priority*.

Intonation

Because Chinese is a tone language speakers are very sensitive to changes of pitch in speech, but they are used to hearing pitch changes over a single syllable, rather than over longer stretches. It may be wise to do some perception practice on tunes extended over a whole clause. Chinese does have intonation, so this area is not as 'new' as may be thought.

Consonant clusters and sequences
HP

Consonant groups are very rare in Chinese; they are therefore a very difficult area.

LS In trying to cope with sequences and clusters, Chinese learners will show the following tendencies:

Word final consonant clusters. These may be simplified by deleting one or more of the consonants. The consonants most often deleted are /r, l, t, and d/, for example 'hold' may become 'ho'.

Word initial consonant clusters. Deletion is also used to simplify these, /r/ seems to be frequently deleted when it follows /p/ or /b/, so 'brothers' may sound like 'bothers'. Other clusters with /r/ ('fr-', 'gr-', etc.) and clusters beginning with /s/ seem not to be so problematic.

Word medial sequences. The consonants most frequently deleted are /r, l, t, d, f, and v/ especially when these sounds occur after a vowel. An example is 'older' which may sound like 'odder'.

Word boundary sequences. One study of learner errors (Anderson, 1983) showed that when three consonants occurred together, the learners deleted at least one of them 95 per cent of the time. In general, sequences at word boundaries were simplified more often than all other types of sequences and clusters. Again the dominant strategy is deletion.

The description of learner strategies clearly shows that vowel insertion is rarely used by Chinese learners to break up consonant groups, and that learners tend to delete one or more of the consonants in a sequence or cluster.

Linkage
HP

Because of the problems with consonants mentioned above, the borders between words are often poorly negotiated. Chinese learners also have a tendency to use glottal stops in words beginning with vowels. These two points conspire to make the speech sound very jerky.

Sources

J. Anderson 'The Difficulties of English Syllable Structure for Chinese ESL Learners' (*Language Learning and Communication* 2 (1) 1983).
Chung-yu Chen 'Pronunciation of English by Students from the Chinese Stream in Singapore' (*Regional English Language Centre Journal* 7/2 1976).
D. Foulds 'The Introduction of English Pronunciation to Cantonese Students' (*The English Bulletin, Hong Kong* 17/1 1978).
Soon Juan Han and Koh Lian Huah 'Aural Discrimination Difficulties of Hong Kong, Malaysian and Singaporean Chinese' (*Regional English Language Centre Journal* (*Singapore*) 7/1 1976).
Mary Tay Wan Joo 'Problems in Teaching Pronunciation' (*Regional English Language Centre Journal* (*Singapore*) 4/1 1973).

French

Rhythm
HP

The rhythm of French is quite different from that of English. French has rhythmic groups, just as English does; it does not have a totally even 'machine gun' rhythm as has sometimes been claimed. The most important feature of rhythm groups in French is that the final syllable of each group is lengthened. For example, in the phrase:

pour l'avenir ('for the future')

the final syllable, 'nir', will last twice as long as 'pour'.
Another characteristic of these phrase-final syllables is that the pitch looks something like this:

that is, the pitch is held level for about the first half of the syllable, and then it falls.

These two features, along with very clear, explicit articulation of the sounds of the final syllable, give it 'prominence' or 'stress'. Another important feature of French rhythm is that unstressed syllables have full vowels. English rhythm is characterized by rhythm groups in which the first syllable is stressed: its consonants and vowels are clearly pronounced, it will be lengthened, and it will be slightly louder than unstressed syllables. The stressed syllable tends to occur at the beginning of the group. The pitch of the stressed syllable is usually higher than that of unstressed syllables – the speaker jumps up in pitch for stressed syllables. Most importantly, the vowels of unstressed syllables are reduced to schwa.

So, in learning English, French speakers must go from a rhythmic pattern which looks basically like this:

to one that looks like this:

To do this, learners must focus on three areas:

1 using reduced vowels in unstressed syllables both before and after the stressed syllable in a phrase or clause

2 moving the focal point of the rhythm group from the end to the beginning of the group

3 jumping up in pitch for stressed syllables.

TS In helping learners to acquire English rhythm, the teacher should:

1 concentrate on the use of reduced vowels in unstressed syllables *leading up to the stressed syllable*

2 give the learners lots of opportunity to practise *following* stressed syllables with weak, unstressed syllables, i.e. making a 'tail' of unstressed syllables.

So, lots of different activities (marking of rhythm, production practice, tapping out rhythmic groups, etc.) should be based on phrases such as the following:

it's im*por*tant to con*si*der the *con*sequences

Word stress
HP

If you look up a word in a French dictionary, the division into syllables will be marked, but there will be no indication that one syllable is stressed and another is not. However, in connected speech, the stress is attracted towards the end of the phrase and therefore to the final syllable of any polysyllabic word. This means that whereas English words tend to have a front-weighting, French words have a tendency for end-weighting. Consequently, French learners, when listening to English, will expect the stressed syllable too late and will be 'surprised' when it falls on the first syllable of the word. The large number of cognate words in French and English make this a particularly difficult area for learners. The mobility of word stress in English is also very problematic.

Problems with consonants
HP/OA

1 /θ/ and /ð/ ('*thin* – *the*') do not occur in French.

LS Learners tend to substitute /s/ and /z/ respectively.

TS See 4.3.3.

HP

2 /tʃ/ and /dʒ/ do not occur ('*check* – *jet*').

LS Learners will tend to substitute /ʃ/ ('*she*') and /ʒ/ ('*rouge*') respectively.

TS Point out that these sounds are a combination of familiar sounds: /t/ + /ʃ/ and /d/ + /ʒ/.

OA

3 /r/.

LS Learners tend to use their 'back r' (some French speakers have a front trilled /r/ and will substitute this).

TS See 4.3.3.

HP

4 /ŋ/ (as in '*sing*') does not occur in French.

HP

5 /h/.

LS Learners tend to misplace /h/, omitting it when it should be pronounced and inserting it where it shouldn't occur.

TS See 4.3.3.

HP 6 /p, t, k/ occur in French, but are not aspirated.

LS Learners tend to produce these sounds in a way that sounds too close to /b, d, g/.

TS See 4.3.3.

LP 7 /t, d, and l/ are produced with the tongue touching the back surface of the front teeth.

Problems with vowels
HP

1 /i/ – /ɪ/ confusion ('b*eat* – b*it*') (/ɪ/ doesn't occur in French).

LS Learners will tend to use /i/ for both vowels.

TS See 4.3.3.

OA 2 /ʊ/ ('b*oo*k') does not occur.

LS Learners tend to use a vowel which is too close to /u/ ('f*oo*d').

Diphthongs
LP 3 /ei/ and /ou/ ('m*ade*' – 's*o*').

LS Learners tend to substitute monothongs for these diphthongs.

HP 4 /ei/ ('s*ay*') may sound too close to /ɛ/ ('p*e*n').

HP 5 /ɔ/ ('c*aw*') may be confused with /ou/ ('s*o*').

HP 6 /a/ – /ʌ/ confusion ('c*a*p – c*u*p').

Intonation

French seems to make less use of gliding pitches than English, preferring instead sudden shifts in pitch between syllables. The distance between pitches seems to be smaller, resulting in what seems to be a generally narrower pitch range.

These are basically differences in detail and should not affect intelligibility. But watch out for the effect of narrow pitch range or evenness in pitch which may result in the learner sounding uninvolved. However, speakers of both languages use high starting pitch to show interest/involvement.

The use of falling-rising tunes seems to be slightly different. Whereas in English ⌣ may show 'something reserved' or be used for mitigation, a very similar pattern in French, ⌣ especially when the rising movement levels off and is held at a middle point, is used to signal 'uncontroversiality' or 'reasonableness' or 'this is not worth fighting over' (i.e. it may be the French way to state shared assumptions). See intonation function 2 in section 4.5.2.

Sentence stress
OA

There is an equivalent to contrastive stress in French which has been called 'accent d'insistance'. The speaker uses extra stress to emphasize or highlight particular words. For example:

l'année der<u>niè</u>re ça s'est <u>très</u> bien passé

is equivalent to:

<u>last</u> year went <u>very</u> well

Learners should respond well to the use of contrastive stress in English. It may be useful to exploit this when trying to teach the stressing of content words (i.e. rhythm) in English.

Linkage
HP

French learners tend to aspirate final /p, t, k/ and to release the tongue contact for final /b, d, g/. This tends to work against smooth linkage of abutting consonants as in 'I want to'. (See Chapter 3 on linkage.)

Sources

M. Kenning 'Intonation Systems in French' (*Journal of the International Phonetic Association* 9/1, 1979).
R. Martineau and J. McGivney *French Pronounciation* (Oxford University Press, 1973).
H. Trocmé 'Les difficultés phonetiques des Français qui apprennent l'anglais' (*IUT Bulletin Pedagogique* 30, 1974)
B. Wenk and F. Wioland 'Is French really syllable-timed?' (*Journal of Phonetics* 10, 1982)

German

Word stress

As far as disyllabic words are concerned, German learners shouldn't have too many problems, because both languages show the same 'front-weighting' tendency.

Like English, German has many suffixes, and some of these determine the stress of a word, so learners should respond to the idea that stress pattern can depend on a suffix. The following is a problem area:

HP

German has four adjectival suffixes which are similar in form to English suffixes:

English	*German*
leg*al*	leg*al*
irrit*able*	irrit*abel*
conserv*ative*	konserv*ativ*
manipul*atory*	manipul*atorisch*

In German, the stress rules for these suffixes are:

-al	stress always on the suffix
-ativ	stress always on -tiv
-abel	stress always on -a-
-atorisch	stress always on -tor-

LS In English, these suffixes are never stressed. Watch out for either of these learner strategies:

1 learners will transfer the German stress rules

2 learners will realize that English suffixes do not work in the same way as their German cognates and devise a general rule, such as: 'Place the stress to the left of the suffix.'

TS Determine which of the strategies learners are using and devise exercises accordingly.

Rhythm
LP

The rhythm of German is very similar to that of English; there should be no problems in this area.

Linkage
LP

In German there are strong and weak forms of words depending on sentence stress placement, so German learners should not find it difficult to adjust to weak forms, although they may need their attention drawn to this feature. Many of the simplifications that occur at word boundaries in English are similar to those that occur in German. For example, in the English phrase 'in case' the 'n' is often pronounced as /ŋ/ because of the influence of the following /k/ sound. In the German phrase 'man kann' ('one can') the same thing happens to the 'n' of 'man'. Learners will automatically use types of simplifications which are appropriate for English.

OA

There is one problem area. In English there is a smooth link between a final consonant in one word and an initial vowel in the next word, as in 'full‿up'. But in German, words beginning in vowels have a preceding glottal stop (a kind of catch in the throat). If this native language habit is carried over into English, the effect will be of too many 'jerks' or slight pauses between words.

Problems with consonants
HP/OA

1 /θ/ and /ð/ ('*th*in – *th*ese') do not occur in German.

LS The most common substitutions are /s/ and /z/ respectively.

TS See 4.3.3.

HP

2 /w/ as in '*w*in' is a problem sound.

LS Learners may confuse this with /v/ or /f/.

TS Compare the sound with /u/ as in 'wh*o*' – tell learners to pronounce the sound as this vowel, saying words like 'wink' as 'u-ink'.

OA

3 /r/.

LS Learners will tend to substitute their native /r/ which will be either too far back or too far forward.

TS See 4.3.3.

HP

4 /b, d, g/.

LS When these sounds occur at the end of a word in English, learners will tend to use /p, t, k/ respectively, so 'bag' may sound like 'back'.

TS Emphasize that final /b, d, g/ are pronounced very 'heavily' in English. Tell learners to imagine there is a vowel after /b, d, g/ but not to pronounce it. Refer to German words like 'Ba*d* – Ba*d*ezimmer' ('bath–bathroom'). In the first word the 'd' will sound like a /t/, in the second it will not (because of the following vowel).

OA

5 German has /tʃ/ ('*ch*oose') but not /dʒ/ ('*j*et').

LS Learners will tend to substitute the former for the latter, and, because the letter 'j' in German represents /j/ as in 'yes', may also substitute /j/ for /dʒ/.

TS Emphasize that /dʒ/ is a 'buzzing' or 'voiced' sound. Also, when the two sounds are at the end of words, point out that the vowel before /tʃ/ should be made very quick and the vowel before /dʒ/ should be lengthened. (This change to the vowels should compensate for the lack of the contrast).

Problems with vowels
HP

1 /ɒ/ as in 'n*o*t' can be problematic.

TS In many parts of Southern Germany, speakers use a vowel very close to this /ɒ/ in words such as 'dann' ('then') and 'wann' ('when'). Ask learners to pronounce one of these German words 'like a South German' would; if the vowel sounds close enough tell them to use that vowel.

HP

2 /a/ – /ɛ/ confusion ('b*a*d – b*e*d').

TS See 4.3.3.

HP

3 /ʌ/ as in 'f*u*n' doesn't occur.

TS Tell learners to make the vowel /ɔ/ as in '*caw*' and smile slightly.

LP

4 *Diphthongs*. Only two diphthongs need to be considered, /ei/ '*say*' and /ou/ '*so*'.

LS Learners will tend to make these as long monothongs.

Note: German has /ə/ '*hatte*' ('had') so production of schwa is no problem, but learners need to be reminded to use it.

Intonation

German learners have relatively few problems in this area. Some learners tend to use a dipping intonation pattern very frequently, especially on stressed words. This can result in what may seem like constant tentativeness in the speech. See functions 3, 4 and 6 in 4.5.2.

Sources

P. Erdmann 'Patterns of Stress Transfer in English and German' (*International Review of Applied Linguistics* XI/3, 1973).
E. Germer *Didaktik der englischen Aussprache* (Hermann Schroedel Verlag KG, 1980).
K. J. Kohler 'Contrastive Sentence Phonology' (*Journal of the International Phonetic Association* 4/2, 1974).

Greek

Problems with consonants
HP

1 /p, t, k/ ('*p*it, *t*ip, *k*it').

These sounds may be produced with not quite enough aspiration. The tendency to aspirate can be cultivated – it is partly present in Greek.

TS (See 4.3.3.) Students can be asked to say Greek names with English-type aspirated stops. The resulting amusement can be quite useful to establish this difference between the two languages. 'Petros', 'Tina', and 'Kate' are three names that can be used. (The Greek pronunciation of these names may sound like 'Betros', 'Dina', and 'Gate' to the English ear.) In Cypriot Greek, these sounds are clearly aspirated in the middle of words – as in the word for 'cat'. It may help to use this word as a demonstration of the target sound.

HP

2 /b, d, g/ ('*b*ig, *d*ig, *g*ig').

These sounds do occur in Greek, but learners may have difficulty in hearing the difference between /d/ and /nd/ and /nt/; between /b/ by itself and /mb/ and /mp/; and between /g/ and /ŋk/ and /ŋg/ (see further details under consonant cluster section following).

LP

3 /r/. The Greek /r/ sound is midway between a 'd-like' sound and a trilled /r/. It is an acceptable substitute for English /r/.

TS The /r/ produced after /p, t, k/ may be too full a sound. If high acceptability is the goal, then learners can be encouraged to soften and reduce it.

HP

4 /m, n, and ŋ/ ('*m*an, *n*o, si*ng*').

LS Learners have a tendency to delete these sounds in certain positions (see full discussion under consonant cluster section following).

HP

5 /j, w/ as in '*y*es' and '*w*ill'.

LS The Greek learner tends to hear and pronounce these two sounds as full vowels (/i/ and /u/ respectively). Although these two sounds are very similar to the consonants* the problem is that /j/ and /w/ pronounced in this way will tend to be interpreted by the English listener as separate syllables. (*Demonstrate this to yourself by saying /i/ as in '*ea*t' followed by '-es' as in '*m*ess'. The result will sound like the word 'yes').
TS Tell the learners to 'shorten' these sounds.

HP

6 /s, ʃ/ ('*S*ue – *sh*oe').

Greek has a sound which is midway between these two English sounds phonetically, so there will be problems in perception and production. The difficulty is compounded by the fact that speakers of some varieties of Greek have a negative stereotype of the /ʃ/ sound, so some Greek learners, particularly those from Athens, may be reluctant to make the sound.

LP
7 /z, ʒ/ ('*zoo, rouge*').

These two sounds will be confused in perception and production.

HP
8 /h/.

LS Greek learners tend to produce this sound with too much force and 'hissing' quality.

TS See 4.3.3.

OA
9 /tʃ/ and /dʒ/ ('*ch*eck – *j*et').

LS Learners often pronounce these like /ts/ as in 'ca*ts*' and /dz/ as in 'fa*ds*'.

TS Work first on the pronunciation of /ʃ, s, z, ʒ/ (problems 6 and 7) and once these are under control, show the learners that /tʃ/ is really a combination of /t/ and /ʃ/ and that /dʒ/ is a combination of /d/ and /ʒ/.

Consonant clusters and sequences

HP
1 Learners have difficulty with the consonant clusters or sequences /mp/, /nt/, and /nk/.

LS Learners frequently mishear and mispronounce the second consonant as /b, d, g/ respectively. For example:

'simple' may be misheard/mispronounced as 'symbol'
'centre' may be misheard/mispronounced as 'sender'
'ankle' may be misheard/mispronounced as 'angle'

HP
2 In words with the clusters or sequences /mb/, /nd/, or /ŋg/ (as in 'si*ng*le'), the learners may delete the first consonant. For example:

'symbol' may be misheard/mispronounced as 'Sybil'
'hand' may be misheard/mispronounced as 'had'
'send' may be misheard/mispronounced as 'said'
'finger' may be misheard/mispronounced as 'figure'

Sometimes these two problems conspire together so that the word 'example' is heard/pronounced as 'exable' (i.e. the /p/ is pronounced as /b/, following 1 and then the /m/ is deleted, following 2). When this happens it can be quite difficult to reconstruct the target word. For example, both 'bend' and 'bent' may be misheard or mispronounced as 'bed'.

TS The problems seem to be slightly less acute when 'mp', 'nd', etc. occur in words as a consonant sequence, (for example, 'impossible' or 'unclear'), because of the words' internal structure of prefix-plus-root. Begin working on these problems using such words, making sure the learners are aware of the prefixes and roots. Then move on to words like 'pump', 'lend', etc. where there is no such structure.

Note: For some learners this problem may manifest itself in the *insertion* of /m, n, or ŋ/ before /b, d, g/, so 'cabbage' may be pronounced as 'cambage'.

LP

3 Greek learners may have difficulty with the cluster 'sm-' as in '*sm*all'. The 's' may be pronounced as a /z/ so 'small' will sound like 'zmall'.

Problems with vowels

1 /i/ – /ɪ/ ('*b*eat – b*i*t') confusion. Greek has one vowel which is midway between these two vowels.

OA

TS In order to establish a contrast, encourage learners to use extreme lip-spreading for /i/.

HP

2 /ɔ/–/ʌ/–/ʊ/ – confusion ('*c*aught – c*u*t – c*oo*k').
  The vowels in this area are very troublesome.

LS Learners may substitute their short 'o' as in 'ios' ('son') for any of these three vowels.

HP

3 There is no schwa in Greek.

LS Learners will substitute either /ɛ/ as in 'b*e*d' or the Greek vowel /a/ as in 'iot*a*' for schwa. The former is a more acceptable substitute.

HP

4 Confusion between /a/ as in 'h*a*t', /ɑ/ as in 'h*a*rd' and /ʌ/ as in 'h*u*t'. This is another troublesome area for learners.

LP

5 Greek has no *diphthongs*, but two vowel sounds can occur in sequence in Greek words.

TS Draw learners' attention to the fact that in Greek they often say two vowels in succession, and that this is basically what they must do to produce English diphthongs. The /ou/ diphthong ('*c*oat') may need special attention.

Rhythm and connected speech

LS Learners may tend to insert a short vowel sound after words which end in a consonant, especially /b, d, g/. For example, 'big' may sound like 'big-a'.

HP

TS This tendency may not be so strong in words that end with /p, t, k/, so work on eliminating this extra vowel from words like 'tip, bit, kick', etc. and then move on to 'need, bid, bag', etc.
  This problem should be given *high priority* because of the possibility of confusion between adjectives and their comparative forms ('big' vs. 'bigger') and verbs and their agentive forms ('keep' vs. 'keeper'). The insertion of vowels at the ends of words can disrupt the rhythm of the learner's speech and affect intelligibility.

Intonation

Learners may have problems with narrow pitch range, so the teacher should monitor this. Other functions of intonation which may cause difficulty are the politeness and mitigation functions (especially the use of high starting pitch to show politeness).

Sources   S. Efstathiades *Greek and English Phonology: a Comparative Investigation* (Thessaloniki 1974).
A. B. Gogos 'Modern Greek Vowels and their Interference in Learning English' (*Views on Language Learning and Language Teaching* Athens 1977).
A. Gordon 'Some Pronunciation Problems: Consonants (*Views on Language and Language Teaching* Athens 1976).

Italian

Problems with consonants

The following English sounds will be 'new' for the Italian learner:

/θ/ as in '*th*ick'
/ð/ as in '*th*at'
/ʒ/ as in 'rou*ge*'
/ŋ/ as in 'si*ng*'

The following list shows the sounds learners may substitute:

HP/OA

1 for /θ/

/f/ as in '*f*un'
/s/ as in '*s*un'
/t/ as in '*t*on'

HP/OA

2 for /ð/

/v/ as in '*v*an'
/z/ as in '*z*oo'
/d/ as in '*d*o'

LP

3 for /ʒ/

/dʒ/ as in '*j*et'

LP

4 for /ŋ/ (word final position)

/n/ as in '*n*o'
/ŋg/ as in 'lo*ng*er'

Note on priorities for 'new' sounds
In dealing with problems 1 and 2 the teacher needs to be more concerned if the learner is substituting /f or v/ and /s or z/ than if /t or d/ is being used. Some English listeners are very used to /t or d/ substitutions; the other substitutions can cause intelligibility problems. Since /ʒ/ is a relatively rare sound, this substitution can be given *low priority*.

Problem 4. /ŋ/ does actually occur in Italian, but only before /k/ and /g/ in words like 'bra*n*co' ('flock') and 'giu*n*gla' ('jungle'). So, the sound becomes fixed in learners' minds as a 'kind of /n/' which only occurs before two of their consonant sounds. If learners substitute /ŋ/ followed by /g/ as in 'lo*ng*er' this is unlikely to cause problems because many accents of English do so as well, and the sequence is phonetically very close to /ŋ/. If the learner substitutes /n/ this may cause word confusions.

OA

5 The sound /h/. Italian learners find it quite easy to acquire and produce this sound, even though it does not occur in Italian, but they may delete /h/ where it should occur, and pronounce it where the letter represents 'silence'. See section 4.3.3.

LP

6 The following English sounds will be pronounced slightly differently by Italian learners, but the differences are minor, and these substitutions will easily be counted the same by the English listener:

/t, d, s, z, n, and l/

LP

7 The Italian /r/ is a trilled or rolled /r/ and learners will tend to use it when they speak English. Its use will sound very 'foreign' to the English ear, but should not affect intelligibility. If learners do want to acquire an 'English /r/', then see 4.3.3.

HP .

8 Italian /p,t, and k/ in initial position do not have the aspiration that these sounds have in English. If the learner uses his Italian /p/ as in the word '*p*enna' for English /p/ as in the word '*p*en', the English listener will probably hear the word as 'Ben'.

HP

9 When learners pronounce the sounds /p,t, and k/ and /b,d, and g/ at the end of words, they will tend to pronounce them very fully and explicitly and to add a very short vowel after the sounds. 'Big' may sound like 'big-a'. This practice can disrupt the rhythm of the speech and can cause intelligibility problems. In particular, it may lead to confusion between agent noun and verb pairs such as 'lead/leader', 'rub/rubber', and comparative and positive forms of adjectives, 'glad/gladder', or 'vague/vaguer'.
TS Encourage the learners not to 'release' these sounds at the ends of words, but to 'freeze', allowing the lips to stay together or the tongue to cling to the roof of the mouth. The teacher will probably have to demonstrate what this sounds like and contrast it with pronunciations that show 'release'.

LP

10 The sound /z/ as in 'zoo' does occur in Italian, but never at the beginning of a word.
LS Learners may tend to pronounce initial 'z' in English words like 'zone', 'zenith' and 'zoo' as /dz/ as in 're*ds*'. This is not a serious problem because there are very few words which begin with /z/ in English.

Problems with vowels

The following vowel sounds do not occur in Italian:

HP

1 /ɪ/ as in 'f*i*t'.

LS Learners tend to substitute /i/ as in 'b*ea*t' for English /ɪ/.

TS It may help to draw the learners' attention to lip shape. The lips are slightly spread for /ɪ/ but have little tension; for /i/ there is a great deal of lip spreading, and more muscular tension.

HP

2 /a/ as in 'm*a*t'.

LS Learners will tend to substitute the sound /ɛ/ as in 'b*e*d' for English /a/, so 'bad' may sound like 'bed'.

TS See the see-saw technique in 4.3.3.

HP 3 /ə/ as in 'about'.

> **LS** Schwa is a difficult sound for Italians, but the difficulty lies not so much in actually managing to produce it as in using it when required. There are two reasons for this:
> (a) There is no weakening of vowels in Italian when they occur in an unstressed syllable.
> (b) Italian learners will tend to pronounce the vowel represented in the spelling of a word, following Italian spelling conventions, which are quite 'phonetic' in the representation of vowels.

OA 4 /ɑ/ as in 'hard'. There *is* a sound in Italian which is phonetically half-way between /a/ and /ɑ/.

> **LS** Learners will tend to use this sound for both /a/ and /ɑ/. Interestingly, the same is true for Scottish English. The words 'Sam' and 'psalm' will rhyme.
>
> **TS** In order to get a vowel sound close to the /ɑ/, refer the learners to the 'word' 'ah' in English, used for showing admiration or understanding.

OA 5 /ʊ/ as in 'book'.

> **LS** Learners may tend to produce this sound with the lips tightly rounded, and with the back of the tongue very close to the position for /k/. So, their vowel will sound too much like /u/ as in 'moon'. Pairs such as 'fool–full' will rhyme.

LP 6 *Diphthongs*. Italian learners will tend to use a long monothong for the diphthong /ou/ as in 'so'.

HP *Vowel length*. There are some important differences in the length of English and Italian vowels. In fact, the conditions which determine how long a vowel is held are virtually mirror images of each other in the two languages, for example:

1 In English, a stressed vowel will be long if it is the final sound in a word, so the vowels in 'true', 'see', 'agree', etc. are longer than the same vowels in 'sooner', 'Peter', etc.

but

1(a) In Italian a stressed vowel tends to be short if it occurs at the end of a word.

2 In English a stressed vowel will 'gain length' if it occurs before the consonants /b, d, g, m, n, l, z/ and will be shorter if it occurs before /p, t, k, tʃ, s/

but

2(a) In Italian, vowels tend to be short if there is a following consonant, no matter what the consonant is.

There are clearly many differences, but the most important results are that:

1 learners may tend to say words ending in a vowel with too short a vowel and

2 they will tend to pronounce words such as 'cab', 'cause', 'mad', with a vowel that is too short.

TS One simple set of rules that can be given to learners is: (1) When there is a vowel at the end of a word, make it very long. (2) When there is a vowel in the middle of a word, say it quickly, unless it is stressed. If the teacher wants to give one general recommendation to learners, then something like the following will be of help:

'Make all your vowels longer.' (If the learner's vowels are overlong, this won't matter as much as if they are too short.)

Rhythm and stress HP	In Italian each syllable in a word is pronounced clearly and distinctly with a full vowel. This applies to both stressed and unstressed syllables. The syllables surrounding the stressed syllable are not 'weakened' as they are in English. Learners will tend to transfer their native language habits to English, and, as a consequence, one important feature that contributes to the characteristic English rhythm will be lacking. In English words where there is a cognate Italian word the tendency will be very strong.
Intonation	Italian learners seem to have relatively few problems with intonation patterns. One feature is noticeable: a tendency for an equal rise-fall on stressed words, particularly at the end of the clause. ⌒ This may have the effect of over-insistence, when this is not the intention.
Consonant clusters and sequences HP	*Word initial clusters.* Italian and English share many initial consonant clusters, but there may be some problems with the following: 1 Clusters beginning with /θ/, such as '*th*rough', '*th*ree' are difficult because this is a new sound.
LP	2 Clusters with a consonant followed by the sound /j/ as in 'yet' or the sound /w/ as in '*w*ill' (examples: 'few', 'twin', 'twig', 'dwell', etc.).
OA	3 Clusters with /r/ as the second element ('pr-', 'tr-', 'br-', 'dr-', etc.) **LS** The learner will probably substitute the Italian /r/ sound for the 'r' in these clusters.
LP	4 Clusters in which /s/ is followed by /l/, /m/, or /n/ (examples: 'sleep', 'smile', 'sneak').

146

LS Learners will transfer a feature of Italian and pronounce the /s/ in these clusters like a /z/.

TS For problem 2 draw the learners' attention to words in Italian beginning with a consonant, followed by the letters 'i' or 'u' and then a vowel. These sequences are extremely close to what must be pronounced in the English words. For example:

Italian	*English*
'fiuto' ('smell')	'few'
'tuono' ('thunder')	'twin'
'duello' ('duel')	'dwell'

For problem 4 get the students to make an exaggerated long /s/ sound and then reduce it gradually (for 'sleep' – /ssslip/→/sslip/→/slip/).
For problem 3 draw the learners' attention to the fact that the clusters 'tr-' and 'dr-' sound very much like the sounds /tʃ/ as in '*cheap*' and /dʒ/ as in '*judge*' respectively. If they use these sounds as substitutes, this may help to reduce the frequency of an Italian trilled /r/ in their speech.

HP

Final clusters. There are no clusters at the end of Italian words, so final clusters in English may cause great difficulties. Clusters with unfamiliar sounds can be even more problematic.

LS Learners will tend to delete consonants. Their tendency to delete single final consonants or to insert a vowel after the consonant (see above) complicates matters.

TS see 4.3.5.

HP

Medial sequences. Learners also have problems with sequences of clusters across word boundaries, and will use the same deletion and vowel insertion strategies.

TS When working on sequences where the same consonant appears at the end of the one word and the beginning of the next, as in 'that time', 'first time', 'deep purple', or 'top people', draw their attention to the fact that there is no 'break' between the two words, and that what English speakers do is make a long consonant sound, just like those that occur in Italian in the middle of words. For example:

'dettame' ('dictate')
'tappo' ('cork')

This may help them to eliminate some of the inserted vowels that affect linkage and cause intelligibility problems.

Word stress
HP

Word stress in Italian is mobile, just as in English, so learners should respond well to the notion that correct placement of stress in a word is important. One problem area centres on the fact that English and Italian have adopted certain suffixes from Latin, but words with these 'cognate' suffixes have different stress patterns.

1 The Italian suffix '-tà' corresponds to the English suffix '-ty'. For example:

Italian   *English*
'abilità'   'ability'
'carità'   'charity'

In Italian, words with this suffix always have the stress on the '-tà':

'abili<u>tà</u>' 'impossibili<u>tà</u>' 'regolari<u>tà</u>'

Watch out for learners wrongly stressing the '-ty' syllable.

2 The Italian suffix '-zione' corresponds to English '-tion'. In Italian words with this suffix the stress falls on '-zion-'; in English the stress falls on the syllable preceding '-tion'.

Italian   *English*
na<u>zione</u>   <u>na</u>tion
rela<u>zione</u>   re<u>la</u>tion

Watch out for learners wrongly stressing '-tion' in English words.

Sources

A. D'Eugenio 'Stress Distribution in Italian and English Words' (*International Review of Applied Linguistics* XV/2 1977).
A. D'Eugenio *Major Problems of English Phonology: with special reference to Italian-speaking Learners* (Foggia: Atlantica 1982).

Japanese

Problems with consonants

1 The following consonants do not occur in Japanese:

HP

/f/ as in 'fan'
/v/ as in 'van'

HP/OA

/ð/ as in 'soothe'
/θ/ as in 'south'

LP

/ʒ/ as in 'rouge' occurs only in combination with the /u/ vowel, so the sequence /ʒu/ as in 'juku' occurs, but not /ʒa/, /ʒo/, etc.

LS Learners will tend to make the following substitutions:

/h/ will be used for /f/, so 'feel' may be pronounced as 'heel'
/z/ or /d/ will be used for /ð/
/s/ or /t/ will be used for /θ/

LP

2 The following consonants occur in Japanese and can be transferred to English with little or no need for modification:

/p, b, t, d, k, g, tʃ (as in 'chip'), dʒ (as in 'Jew'), s, z, ʃ (as in 'shoe'), m, n, ŋ (as in 'ringer'), w, j (as in 'yet'), h/

However, some of these consonants only occur before particular vowels in Japanese, so learners may have problems when they try to pronounce an 'unfamiliar' consonant-vowel sequence. Here are some potential trouble spots:

(a) The sequences /ti/ and /tu/ don't occur in Japanese. Watch out for problems with words like 'team', 'two', etc.

(b) The sequence /si/ doesn't occur. Watch for problems with 'see', 'seat', 'seed', etc.

(c) /ʃ/ doesn't occur before /ɛ/ as in 'bed' or /ei/ as in 'made'; possible problem words will be 'shade', 'shell', 'shame', etc.

(d) The only vowel which commonly follows /w/ as in 'wet' in Japanese is /a/, so whereas 'whack' will not be a problem, 'win', 'wait', 'would', 'we', etc. may be.

(e) The Japanese /h/ sounds very much like /ʃ/ as in 'shoe' when it occurs before the vowel /i/, so in English, learners' pronunciation of the word 'he' may sound like 'she'. What looks like a grammatical difficulty may result from this pronunciation problem. Also, the sequence /hu/ does not occur, so learners' pronunciation of the word 'who' may sound like 'foo'.

(f) Japanese /b/ may sometimes be pronounced almost like a /v/, so in English this may lead to a /v/-/b/ confusion.

149

Note: In final or medial position, the sounds /p, t, and k/ may be pronounced with excessive aspiration. This may result, for example, in /t/ sounding like /tʃ/ to the English ear – 'eating' would sound like 'each-ing'.

HP   3 /l/ – /r/ confusion. Japanese speakers often cannot distinguish English /r/ from /l/. They will tend to use a sound which sounds most like an /l/ to the English listener, although at times the substituted sound may be a /d/ ('resign' may sound like 'design').

TS See 4.3.3.

LP   4 /z/ in final position may be a problem – it may be pronounced more like /s/.

Problems with vowels

Japanese has five vowels; learners will probably have quite a few problems with the much larger English vowel system.

HP   1 /ɪ/ ('p*i*t') /i/ ('P*e*te'). The first of these doesn't occur in Japanese, but the second does.

LS Learners will tend to substitute the /i/ for the /ɪ/ vowel, so 'sit' may sound like 'seat'.

HP   2 Schwa does not occur in Japanese.

LS Learners tend to substitute many different vowels for /ə/.

OA   3 Japanese has an /u/ as in 'm*oo*n', but no /ʊ/ as in 'f*oo*t'. Word pairs such as 'suit – soot' will be confused.

LS Learners will tend to use their /u/ vowel in words like 'foot', 'book', etc.

HP   4 Japanese has a vowel which is fairly close to /a/ as in 'c*a*p', but there may be confusion between /a/ in 'c*a*p', /ʌ/ in 'c*u*p', and /ɑ/ as in 'h*a*rd'.

LS Learners may substitute /ɔ/ for /ɑ/ so that 'odd' will be pronounced to rhyme with 'awed'.
TS Japanese has what are called 'double vowels'; two identical vowels in succession are pronounced as a long vowel equal in length to two vowels of normal length. The double vowel /a–a/ in Japanese can be used as a satisfactory substitute for the English /ɑ/ as in 'hard'.

OA   5 If learners have problems with the /ei/ vowel, as in 'g*a*te', draw their attention to the fact that they have a vowel very close to this in words with the double vowel /e–e/. Examples are:

'eega' ('movie')
'seeji' ('politics')
'ee' ('yes')

OA   6 Japanese has a vowel which is close to both /ɒ/ as in 'n*o*t' and /ɔ/ as in '*law*'. Learners may have difficulty distinguishing pairs such as 'cot' and 'caught'.

OA

7 If learners have problems with the vowel in '*coat*' and '*note*', they can use one of their 'double vowels'. Two words that have this vowel are 'ooyo' ('apply') and 'ookii' ('big'); these words can be used to demonstrate to learners that they have an adequate substitute for this vowel in English.

OA

8 Learners *may* have problems with the /ɛ/ as in 'qu*e*stions'. Substitutions may include a sound in the /i/–/ɪ/ area or /ei/ as in '*A*pril'.

Rhythm and stress
HP

In Japanese each syllable is given equal stress, so a word of four syllables will take twice as long to pronounce as a word of two syllables. Learners may have great difficulty with the characteristic rhythm of English with its alternation of stressed and unstressed syllables. It is interesting to note how *English*-speakers cope with familiar Japanese names. Hiroshima is alternatively pronounced with stress on '-ro-' or on '-shi-', but the Japanese pronunciation has equal stress on each of the four syllables. Likewise, the Japanese learner may pronounce 'Birmingham' as 'Ba – ming – ham' with equal stress on each syllable.

Mistakes in placement of stress in words and in sentences are frequent. (The latter arises because of the difficulties learners have in understanding the link between stress placement and meaning in sentences.)

Weak forms
HP

Because of the lack of a schwa vowel, and because of the problems with the rhythmic and stress features of English, learners will have difficulties in the use of weak forms of words.

LS Learners will fail to 'obscure' the vowel to schwa in unstressed syllables, and will use a full vowel. They will also expect each consonant to be pronounced explicitly and clearly, and will be unlikely to use – or recognize – elisions of consonants and changes that occur to some consonants (i.e. the 'blurrings' of connected speech).

Consonant clusters and sequences
HP

Japanese has very few clusters of consonants. The normal patterns of syllables are C-V-C-V or C-V-V (the latter in syllables with the 'double vowels'). So sequences and clusters of consonants in English will cause difficulties.

LS The dominant strategy is to insert vowels between consonants to break up the cluster. The learner may pronounce 'screw' as 'su-ku-ru'. In words or syllables that end with a consonant, a vowel may be inserted after the final consonant as well, so 'steak' may be pronounced as 'su-te-ki'.

Intonation

Intonation may well be less of a problem for learners than the features of rhythm and stress, and consonants and vowels. It has been observed that in Japanese the transitions between pitch levels seem to be more abrupt than in English, but if this feature is transferred to English this will not lead to unacceptable patterns.

151

Because the pitch of the voice functions to signal stress there may be difficulties in synchronizing pitch change with the main stress in the sentence.

There is also another area of potential difficulty, and this relates to overall pitch level or pitch 'range'. When expressing politeness in Japanese, women tend to use much higher overall pitch than Japanese men. In other words pitch level of the voice separates the sexes in Japanese. This is not the case in English. When expressing politeness English men *and* women use high overall pitch. So in Japanese, a high overall pitch is used to express a stereotypically female role. Japanese men emphasize the masculinity of their speech by adopting a deep-voiced mode of speaking which is often accompanied by stiff postures and stern faces. This may go some way to explaining the remark of a Japanese male learning English who said how 'feminine' he felt when intoning politely in English (Loveday, 1981). The teacher should watch out for use of low overall pitch range by male Japanese learners when the higher part of the pitch range is needed to convey politeness. But extremely tactful encouragement may be needed, and if there is little improvement in this area, it may be best to suggest that male speakers compensate for low pitch by smiles and the use of polite phrases/expressions. Low pitch can sound very sincere, if it is accompanied by appropriate gestures and facial expressions.

Sources

Isamu Ibe 'Intonation Patterns in Japanese' in D. Bolinger *Intonation* (Penguin 1972).
Kimizuka Sumako *Teaching English to Japanese* (Tail Feather, Moab, Utah 1977).
L. Loveday 'Pitch, politeness, and sexual role' (*Language and Speech* 24 1981).

Spanish

**Problems with
consonants**
HP

1 Confusion between /b/ and /v/ ('*b*an – *v*an').

LS There is a sound in Spanish which is a kind of combination of /b/ and /v/. Learners tend to substitute this sound for the two English consonants.

TS Draw learners' attention to the fact that for /b/ the lips should start out very tightly closed and then this closure is quickly released, and that for /v/ the lower lip should touch the upper teeth.

HP

2 /d/ may be too close to /ð/ as in '*th*en' so the word '*d*ay' sounds like '*th*ey'.

TS Emphasize the definite contact between tongue and roof of the mouth needed as a starting position for /d/, and the sound's quick release.

HP

3 /θ/ as in '*th*in' is absent in some varieties of Spanish. Watch out for /f/ as in '*f*in' or /s/ as in '*s*in' as substitutes.

HP

4 /s/ and /z/ ('*s*ue–*z*oo'). In some varieties these two sounds do not occur. Learners may delete these sounds, use /s/ for both /s/ and /z/, or replace either or both sounds with a kind of /h/ sound, so 'Sue' could sound like 'hue'.

HP

5 /ʃ/ as in '*sh*oe'. This sound does not occur in many varieties.

LS Learners tend to substitute either /tʃ/ as in '*ch*eck' or /s/ as in 'Sue'. If learners are able to produce the sound, they may actually overuse it, and use /ʃ/ where /tʃ/ should occur, eg '*ch*erry' will be pronounced as '*sh*erry'.

LP

6 /dʒ/ and /ʒ/ ('*j*et – plea*s*ure'). /dʒ/ is an unfamiliar sound, and learners will either substitute /tʃ/ as in '*ch*eck' or the sound represented by the letter 'y' in Spanish (as in the word 'yuyo'). The latter will sound foreign, but will still be intelligible. This Spanish sound may also be used for /ʒ/.

HP

7 /j/ as in '*y*et'.

LS Learners will either use the Spanish sound mentioned in 6 as a substitute or they may substitute /dʒ/ as in '*j*et', so '*y*ell' may sound like 'gel'.

HP

8 /w/ as in '*w*et'.

LS Learners may pronounce this as a /b/ or they may insert a /g/ before the sound, so '*w*ent' may sound like 'Gwent'.

HP

9 /p/ ('*p*at') and /k/ ('*k*it').

153

LS Speakers of some South American varieties may not use sufficient aspiration for /p/ and may tend to delete /k/ at the end of a word.

HP   10 /h/ as in 'hold'.

LS Learners will either delete the sound where it should be pronounced or pronounce it with a great deal of 'hissing' quality. There may also be confusion between /h/ and /dʒ/, so 'ham' may sound like 'jam'.

TS See 4.3.3.

LP   11 /r/.

LS Learners will substitute their native sound, which is a trill or /d/-like sound. Both are acceptable, but will sound foreign. Encourage learners to adopt an 'r-less' style of pronunciation.

12 /ŋ/ as in 'sing'.

LS In the middle of words, e.g. in 'bank', this sound will cause no problems; at the end of words, the learner may:

LP   (a) pronounce the /g/, so the word 'sing' will end with a consonant cluster

HP   (b) substitute /n/ as in 'no', so 'wing' may be pronounced as 'win'. Strategy (b) will cause more intelligibility problems than (a).

Consonant clusters and sequences   Spanish and English share many clusters, so learners cope quite well except when the English cluster contains an unfamiliar sound. The following are problem areas:

HP   1 Two- and three-element clusters beginning with /s/ ('small, slow, scream', etc.)

LS Learners may insert a vowel before the /s/, so 'small' sounds like 'a-small'.

TS The sequence /s/ plus a consonant does occur in Spanish across syllable boundaries. See 4.3.5.

LP   2 Learners will tend to add /s/ for noun plurals, even where /z/ is required, so 'pens' will sound like 'pence'.

HP   3 Final consonant clusters with /s/ are generally no problem ('picks, bets', etc.) But speakers of some varieties may delete the final /s/.

HP   4 Final consonant clusters with /t/ and /d/ are problematic ('test', 'laughed'). Learners may delete the final /t/ or /d/ or insert a vowel between the two consonants, resulting in forms like 'laugh-ed' or 'laugh'.

HP   5 The combination /s/ plus consonant plus /s/ is a difficult one ('nests', 'risks').

LS The usual escape route is to delete one of the two /s/'s.

TS See 4.3.5.

Word stress

HP

One area of difficulty is the stress of compound words and adjective + noun combinations. English has forms such as:

<u>black</u>bird (stress on the first element)
white <u>house</u> (stress on the second element)
<u>white</u> house (stress on the first element to show emphasis or contrast)

With rare exceptions, Spanish has no equivalent compounding structures. Learners fail to sense the distinction between <u>x</u> x and x <u>x</u> pairs, confusing both groups into one understood as <u>x</u> x. Word order is used to achieve what is accomplished by stress placement in English.

TS Draw learners' attention to the fact that English adjective-noun structures with stress on the noun are equivalent to Spanish adjective-noun phrases:

new <u>book</u>   (nuevo libro)   old <u>friend</u>   (viejo amigo)

and Spanish noun-adjective phrases bear an overwhelming similarity to English 'contrastive' structures:

<u>new</u> book   (libro nuevo)   <u>old</u> friend   (amigo viejo)

This may help persuade learners that they need to pay attention to stress placement.

Sentence stress
HP

Many meanings which are conveyed in English through sentence stress are conveyed in Spanish through particular words. For example, in English (a) 'I have some <u>books</u>' conveys the idea that the possession of books is the most important part of the message, whereas (b) 'I have <u>some</u> books' means that the quantity of books is the point of information focus. Spanish would convey these two different meanings through the words 'unos' and 'algunos'. The Spanish equivalent of (a) is. 'Tengo unos libros', and of (b) 'Tengo algunos libros'. Similarly, where English uses stress to reassert or reaffirm (for example, 'I <u>can</u> do that') Spanish uses the word ('sí').

Intonation

There seem to be three areas that need attention:

1 *Pitch range.* Spanish speakers seem to use too narrow a pitch range. Where English speakers will start quite high and finish fairly low in their range, perhaps hitting extreme pitches within a phrase as well, Spanish speakers keep to a much more restricted pitch movement over a phrase or clause.

2 *Final falling pitch movement* (for example, on statements or last items in a list). The final falling pitch may not sound low enough. This may be due to the fact that Spanish speakers rarely use a slight rise before the final falling pitch, which makes the final pitch movement sound too 'flat'.

3 *The rise-fall seems difficult.* This may be because the pitch-reversal itself is difficult for learners to do, especially on short phrases or one syllable ('Oh' or 'Wonderful idea!') or because of shyness or self-consciousness.

Problems in areas 1 and 3 may result in learners failing to convey 'involvement' or 'interest' in conversations with English speakers, who seem to use wide pitch range and extreme pitch reversals to signal 'interest' or 'involvement' in the topic of conversation.

Problems with vowels

HP

1 /ei/ – /ɛ/ ('*a*ges-*e*dges') confusion.

    TS Encourage the learners to use lip spreading for /ei/.

HP

2 /ʌ/ ('b*u*t') does not occur in Spanish.

    LS Learners may substitute a sound that is similar to /o/ making 'm*u*st' sound like 'm*o*st', or /a/ so it sounds like 'm*a*st'·

HP

3 /ɪ/ – /i/ ('b*i*t – b*ea*t') confusion.

    LS Learners will use the latter for both vowels.

HP

4 /a/ – /ɛ/ confusion ('b*a*t – b*e*t').

    LS Learners will tend to use the latter for both vowels.

OA

5 /u/ – /ʊ/ ('b*oo*t – b*oo*k') confusion.

    LS The former will be used by most learners for both vowels.

HP

6 /ə/ does not occur in Spanish.

    LS Learners will substitute the vowel suggested by the spelling.

HP

7 There is no variation in length in Spanish vowels.

    LS Learners will tend to make vowels equally long, which will be too short for the English ear.

    TS Give a general recommendation to lengthen vowels.

Sources

N. Backman 'Intonation Errors in 8 Second Language Spanish-speaking Adults' (*Interlanguage Studies Bulletin* 4/2 1979).
M. Dresden 'English Consonant Clusters and the Spanish-speaking Learner' (*English Language Journal* 3/3 1972).
D. W. Foster 'A Contrastive Note on Stress and Equivalent Structures in Spanish' (*International Review of Applied Linguistics* 6/3 1968).
S. Pollock 'English Prosodics – a Contrastive Approach' (*Modern Language Journal* 62/8 1978).

Turkish

<table>
<tr><td>Problems with consonants</td><td>Turkish shares many consonants with English, so learners have relatively few 'new' sounds to cope with.</td></tr>
<tr><td>HP/OA</td><td>1 /θ/ ('thick') and /ð/ ('that') do not occur in Turkish.</td></tr>
</table>

Problems with consonants

Turkish shares many consonants with English, so learners have relatively few 'new' sounds to cope with.

HP/OA

1 /θ/ ('*th*ick') and /ð/ ('*th*at') do not occur in Turkish.

LS Learners will tend to substitute either /s/ or /t/ for /θ/, so 'thick' may sound like 'sick' or 'tick'. /z/ or /d/ will be substituted for /ð/ so 'that' will sound like 'zat' or 'dat'.

TS See 4.3.3.

HP

2 /v/ ('*v*et') and /w/ ('*w*et') may be confused perceptually and in production.

LS It may be particularly difficult for learners to produce /v/ before vowels such as '*v*ote', '*v*oice' and '*v*olume'. Establish words like 'vet', 'view', 'vat', etc. first and then move on to the more difficult words. It may help to tell the learners that /w/ is really very similar to the vowel /u/ as in 'm*oo*n'.

HP

3 Words *ending with* /b, d, g, and dʒ/ (as in '*j*ud*ge*').

LS Learners may tend to substitute /p, t, k, and tʃ/ (as in '*ch*eck') respectively.
Learners will not have as much difficulty in hearing the difference between, say, 'mat' and 'mad' as in producing it.

TS It may help if learners make a very long vowel before any word with a /b, d, g, or dʒ/ sound (for example, 'mad' should be pronounced 'm-a-a-a-d').

HP

4 In words in which /p, t, k, and tʃ/ ('*ch*eck') occur in the middle (i.e. between vowels) learners may tend to substitute /b, d, g, and dʒ/ respectively, so 'butter' may sound like 'budder'.

LP

5 Turkish /r/ is an adequate substitute for English /r/, but when it occurs at the end of a word, learners may tend to pronounce it with a 'hissing' quality. It may sound like a whispered /r/. If this is a strong feature of the accent, it may be useful to encourage the learner to adopt an 'r-less' style of pronunciation. This will reduce the number of r's.

OA

6 Words with /ŋ/ as in 'si*ng*'.

LS Learners will tend to insert either a /g/ or a /k/ sound. This means that a word like 'sing' will be pronounced with a final consonant cluster (as in some accents of English) and that the '-ing' ending may sound like the word 'ink', so 'singing' may sound like 'sing–gink'.

TS If learners consistently pronounce '-ing' endings as 'ink' it may help to point out that English people often pronounce words like 'going' as 'go in'.

Although these pronunciations are considered to be very informal, this may be preferable to an 'ink' pronunciation, which English listeners may find comical, even irritating. Depending on the scale of the problem, it may be worth considering this strategy.

Problems with vowels HP	1 The /ɪ/ – /i/ contrast ('p*i*t – P*e*te') is troublesome. **LS** Learners will use /i/ for both vowels.
HP	2 The /a/ vowel as in 'c*a*t'. This vowel occurs in Turkish, but only next to certain consonants. Learners may have difficulty in producing this vowel in some English words, but not in others. The vowel may also be confused with /ɑ/ as in 'b*a*rn' or /ʌ/ as in 'b*u*t'. **TS** Use Turkish 'alt' ('bottom') as a help word for this vowel (or any Turkish word written with the symbol 'â' with a circumflex).
OA	3 The /ɔ/ – /ɒ/ ('n*au*ghty – n*o*t') contrast. **LS** Learners may use a vowel which is closer to /ɑ/ as in 'h*a*rd' for both vowels.
OA	4 The /ʊ/ – /u/ ('f*u*ll – f*oo*l') contrast is problematic. **LS** Learners will tend to use a vowel which is close to /u/ for both vowels.
HP	5 /ə/. Although schwa does not exist in Turkish, there is a Turkish vowel which is an adequate substitute. The letter symbol for this vowel is 1 (it resembles a numeral one in form). **TS** Ask the learners for Turkish words using this symbol, and then tell them they can use this for English schwa. Even though producing schwa will not be too difficult, remembering to use it in unstressed syllables will require work and attention.
HP	6 Diphthongs *may* be a serious problem, since there are no diphthongs in Turkish. In particular the /ei/ as in 'p*ay*' is troublesome because it may be confused with /ɛ/ as in 'b*e*t'.
HP	7 In certain positions in Turkish the vowels virtually disappear. If this habit is carried over to English, then a word like 'city' may 'lose' its first vowel and sound like 'stee'. In general, all vowels tend to be pronounced too short. **TS** Give learners a general instruction to 'lengthen vowels.'
Consonant clusters and sequences	1 There are no initial consonant clusters in Turkish; therefore, words in English with two or three consonants will be difficult. The most problematic seem to be those in which the first consonant is /s/.

HP	**LS** Learners will often insert a vowel before or after the /s/, so 'stone' may sound like 'i-stone' or 'si-tone'. Other initial clusters seem to cause fewer problems because of the recent borrowed words from English. For example, 'tr-' and 'fl-' should be easy for learners because the words for 'train' ('tren') and 'flute' ('flavta') have been borrowed.
OA	2 Turkish has many of the same final clusters as English. However, two-term clusters in which the second consonant is /b, d, g/ may cause difficulties because of the tendency to replace these sounds by /p, t, k/. (See section on consonants). Three-term final clusters ('against', 'doesn't', etc.) may also cause problems. **TS** See 4.3.5.

Word stress

HP

Word stress in Turkish is mobile, as it is in English, so learners should not be too bothered by shifting stress in English words. However, there are some tendencies in Turkish, which, if carried over into English, may lead to incorrect placement of stress. These are as follows:

1 A large number of words in Turkish, including all proper names, all verbs, adverbs, conjunctions and pronouns, have stress on the last syllable. This conflicts with a strong tendency in English for 'front-weight' in polysyllabic words.

2 Adjectives usually have stress on the first syllable. If learners use a strategy based on this for English they will correctly stress many adjectives (for example, 'pretty', 'little', 'lovely', etc.), but watch out for wrong stress placement on 'expensive', 'excessive', etc.

3 In Turkish negative sentences, the syllable before the negative suffix is stressed. This may result in English negative sentences which sound (unintentionally) over-insistent. ('He isn't coming.')

Rhythm

HP

Turkish has a much more even rhythm than English does. Learners have a tendency to pronounce each syllable as clearly and explicitly as any other. There is no squeezing of unstressed syllables between stressed ones as in English. These tendencies, and the problem of remembering to use schwa, make appropriate rhythm difficult for learners to achieve.

Sentence stress

LP

Turkish learners should have relatively few problems with placement of stress in sentences. Learners will carry over, with positive results, their tendency to stress content words, and to destress 'repeated' or 'old' information.

Intonation

There seem to be relatively few problems here, but the teacher may notice two areas of difficulty:

1 In English a slight rise in pitch is often used for repeated information –
   Turkish learners may not use this appropriately.

2 There may be difficulties with the fall-rise tune, especially when it is
   telescoped into one syllable, as in 'Don't you like him?' 'Well, not really, but
   I like his friend.' This may be due to shyness or to the feeling that this is an
   'exaggerated' pitch change.

Source   Huseyin Irkad 'Techniques to be Involved in Teaching English Pronunciation
to Turkish Learners' (unpublished dissertation, University of Edinburgh
1972).

Suggestions for further reading

All publications referred to below are listed in the Bibliography.

1
General works with relevant chapters/sections

General works on teaching English as a foreign/second language which have chapters on pronunciation are Abbott and Wingard 1981; Rivers and Temperley 1978; and Stevick 1982.

2
Descriptions of the English sound system

Two very detailed descriptions of English pronunciation are Roach 1983 and Gimson 1980. Gimson has an appendix on Teaching the Pronunciation of English, which not only gives a good overview of the basic issues, but discusses priorities in teaching sounds. Roach has useful accompanying taped material.

3
Phonetic theory and transcription

For those interested in learning more about phonetics, Ladefoged 1982 is recommended. The treatment is very comprehensive, and there are exercises for each topic. (*Note*: The later chapters are concerned with highly theoretical issues. Chapter 5 is an excellent introduction to word stress, sentence stress, and intonation.) Wells and Colson 1971 is much shorter, and particularly useful for learning phonetic transcription.

4
Sources of practice material

For the area of sounds, Baker 1981 and 1982 are very useful as is Ponsonby 1982. Mortimer 1984 is a good source of material for rhythm, linkage, and clusters.

For intonation Cook 1979 has many useful activities. Haycraft and Lee 1982 is a good source of dialogue-based activities.

For word stress, Poldauf 1984 is recommended as a source of examples. It is an extremely detailed analytical study but a comprehensive index makes it very valuable as a source of words which follow particular patterns.

5
Sound simplifications and linkage

Brown 1977 has a very valuable account of the processes of simplification in speech; O'Connor 1967 has a useful section (p 117–20).

Bibliography

ABBOTT, G and WINGARD, P *The Teaching of English as an International Language* (Collins 1981)

ADAMS, C *English Speech Rhythm and the Foreign Learner* (Mouton 1979)

BAKER, A *Introducing English Pronunciation* (Cambridge University Press 1982)

BAKER, A *Ship or Sheep?* 2nd edition (Cambridge University Press 1981)

BAKER, A *Tree or Three?* (Cambridge University Press 1982)

BRAZIL, D, COULTARD, M and JOHNS, C *Discourse Intonation and language teaching* (Longman 1980)

BROWN, G *Listening to Spoken English* (Longman 1977)

BYRNE, D *Teaching Oral English* (Longman 1986)

COOK, V *Using Intonation* (Longman 1979)

GIMSON, A *An Introduction to the Pronunciation of English* 3rd edition (Edward Arnold 1980)

HAYCRAFT, B and LEE W *It Depends How You Say It* (Pergamon 1982)

HOLE, J 'Pronunciation Testing – What did you say?' (*English Language Teaching Journal* 37/2 1983)

HUBICKA, O 'Why bother about phonology?' (*Practical English Teaching* I/1 1980)

HUBICKA, O Phonology: stress (*Practical English Teaching* I/3 1981)

LADEFOGED, P *A Course in Phonetics* 2nd edition (Harcourt, Brace, Jovanovich 1982)

MACCARTHY, P *The Teaching of Pronunciation* (Cambridge University Press 1978).

MAXWELL, C *The Pergamon Dictionary of Perfect Spelling* 2nd edition (Pergamon 1978)

MC ARTHUR, T and HELIEL, M *Learning Rhythm and Stress* (Collins 1974)

MORRIS, T 'Topic and focus of information: some implications for the teaching of main sentence stress' (*World Language English* 3/2 1984)

MORTIMER, C *Elements of Pronunciation* (Cambridge University Press 1984)

O'CONNOR, J *Better English Pronunciation* (Cambridge University Press 1967)

OSKARSSON, M *Approaches to Self-assessment in Foreign Language Learning* (Pergamon 1980)

POLDAUF, I *English Word Stress* (Pergamon 1984)

PONSONBY, M *How now, brown cow?* (Pergamon 1982)

RIVERS, W *Hearing and Comprehending: Teaching foreign language skills* revised edition (University of Chicago Press 1980)

RIVERS, W and TEMPERLEY, M *A Practical Guide to the Teaching of English as a second or foreign language* (Oxford University Press 1978)

ROACH, P *English Phonetics and Phonology* (Cambridge University Press 1983)

STEVICK, E *Teaching and Learning Languages* (Cambridge University Press 1982)

STREVENS, P *Teaching English as an International Language* (Pergamon 1980)

STUBBS, M *Language and Literacy* (Chapter 5 on spelling) (Routledge and Kegan Paul Ltd 1980)

THOMPSON, I 'Who needs intonation?' (*World Language*) *English* 2/1 1982)

WELLS, J and COLSON, G *Practical Phonetics* (Pitman 1971).

Index